Auxilia Graeca: Containing Forms Of Parsing And Greek Trees, The Greek Prepositions, Rules Of Accentuation, Greek Idioms, Etc.

Hugh Fowler

AUXILIA GRÆCA:

CONTAINING

FORMS OF PARSING AND GREEK TREES,

THE GREEK PREPOSITIONS,

RULES OF ACCENTUATION,

GREEK IDIOMS, &c. &c.

For the Use of Schools.

BY THE REV. HUGH FOWLER, M.A.

LATE FELLOW OF SIDNEY SUSSEX COLLEGE, CAMBRIDGE,

HEAD MASTER OF THE COLLEGE SCHOOL,

GLOUCESTER.

LONDON:

BELL AND DALDY.

MDCCCLVI.

Gloucester: Printed by Edward Power, Westgate Street.

PREFACE.

THIS little work is designed chiefly for schools in which Wordsworth's Grammar is used, and is meant to be *auxiliary* and supplementary to it. It may, however, be easily adapted to any other good Grammar. The forms of Parsing (Part I.) have been used for many years by the Author with his pupils, and have been found effective in producing fluent and accurate parsing. They may be used either *vivâ voce*, or for written exercises. For the latter purpose, chiefly, the lists of words for parsing have been added. The plan recommended for parsing *in class*, is to make each boy in succession take up the sections into which the forms are divided. After a little practice this will go on with great rapidity, and the Master need do little more than interfere now and then to correct a mistake.

Part II. contains forms of Greek Trees for each of the five Conjugations, with lists of words for Trees. It is desirable—at least for the more advanced boys—that they should have at hand some good Catalogue of Greek verbs, and when they set down any tenses, which appear, from the Catalogue, not to be in general use, to prefix a (*) to them.†

In Part III. a list of the irregular verbs in most frequent use is given, with their principal tenses.

---

† Baird's " Catalogue of Greek Verbs," published by Longman, is copious and accurate.

The object of Part IV. is to smooth the difficulties of the Greek Prepositions for beginners. The subject is well and copiously treated by Wordsworth, but it has been found in practice that the nice distinctions of meaning, when presented to a boy in a Latin dress, are not readily comprehended, or easily committed to memory. The Author at first intended merely to translate Wordsworth's *Syntaxis Præpositionum*, but he changed his plan, and, after consulting the best of the larger Grammars, especially Jelf's and Arnold's, and Madvig's Syntax, arranged his notes in their present form. He hopes he has succeeded in making the explanations as simple as possible, without omitting anything of importance. He has endeavoured to select the shortest and most striking examples.

Part V. is a treatise on the Greek accents. The three pages devoted to this most important, though sadly-neglected, branch of Greek scholarship, in Wordsworth's Grammar, terse and admirable as his rules are, cannot be otherwise than very defective. The Author ventures to hope that the 100 rules he has given will enable a boy to accent most of the Greek words in his exercises, without the necessity of referring to his Lexicon. He is largely indebted to Goettling (*Allgemeine Lehre vom Accent, &c.*, Jena, 1835) as also to Jelf and Arnold.

Part VI. contains a few of the more common Greek Idioms, extracted partly from Arnold's school books. Jelf, Matthiæ, and Madvig have also been consulted. It is intended that boys should commit to memory the passages quoted as illustrations. It is obvious that this part might have been extended to a very great length, and the Author's chief difficulty has been the selection of the *most useful* Idioms and Constructions, and those of most constant occurrence.

CONTENTS.

CONTENTS.

ERRATA.

Page 3. line 1, for Κυρος...................... read Κῦρος.
— 4. line 6, (from bottom), for Ἑλληνες...... „ Ἑλληνες.
— 6. line 7, for λάβε..................... „ λαβὲ.
— 8. line 5, for γύναικα .... „ γυναῖκα.
—— Ex. 2. 5, for θεντὸς (bis.) .... „ θέντος.
—— Ibid. „ for θεντὶ (bis.).............. „ θέντι.
—— Ex. 3. 1 (and p. 9, 5), for λαθούσαι .... „ λαθοῦσαι.
— 13. Ex. 3. 5, for γύναικι .... „ γυναικὶ
— 14. Ex. 2. 1, for ῃσι .... „ ᾖσι.
—— Ibid. 3, for ου (bis.) .... „ οὖ.
—— Ibid. for φ, ῃ, φ .... „ ᾦ, ᾖ, ᾧ.
—— Ibid. for ων (ter.).................... „ ὦν.
— 17. Ex. 3. for ῃν .... „ ἦν.
— 30. 52, for ἀπεθώνμαζε .... „ ἀπεθωύμαζε.
— 35. § 6. 5, for δημοσίᾳ................. „ δημοσίᾳ.
— 36. 24, for ψευδείαις..................... „ ψευδεῖς.
— 55. line 1, for ευρον..................... „ εὖρον.
— 62. line 5, for δυο .... „ δύο.
—— Ibid. for ων .... „ ὦν,
— 66. line 3, for γὴν .... „ γῆν.
— 69. line 4 (from bottom), for τον .... „ τὸν.
— 76. I. d. for **Though** .... „ **Through.**
—— II. a. for Τρωας .... „ Τρῶας.
— 94. 9, 3, for ανθρωπος .... „ ἄνθρωπος.
— 101. 43, for πεποιησθαι .... „ πεποιῆσθαι.

PART I.

FORMS OF PARSING.

I. *Form of Parsing Regular Verbs.*

§ 1. Verbs in ω.

1. Say from what Verb it comes—Voice (if Deponent, whether of the Passive or Middle Form)—Mood—Tense—Number—Person.

2. Describe the Verb—state its Conjugation, and the Characteristics of the Conjugation (if a Contract Verb, state to which Formation of Contracts it belongs)—give the Root according to the Rules in § 70, of Gr. Gr.—Principal Tenses, viz. Future, Perfect Active, Perfect Passive, First Aorist Passive.

3. Rule for Formation of the Tense (and, if required, of all the Tenses that lead up to the Tense in question.)

4. Cognate Tenses.

5. Go through the Tense until you come to the word.

6. State the Agreement or Government of the Verb, and give the Rule in either case.

EXAMPLES.

Ex. 1. To parse the verb ἐκρύφθησαν.

1. ἐκρύφθησαν is a Verb from κρύπτω—Passive Voice—Indicative Mood—First Aorist Tense—Plural Number—Third Person.

B

2. κρύπτω is a Verb in ω of the First Conjugation (Characteristics, π, β, φ, πτ)—Root *κρύβω ("πτ fit β ") κρύψω, κέκρυφα, κέκρυμμαι, ἐκρύφθην.

3. " Aoristum Primum Passivum," &c. (§ 64, Gr. Gr.)

4. ἐκρύφθην; κρύφθητι, κρυφθῶ, κρυφθείην, κρυφθῆναι, κρυφθείς.

5. ἐκρύφθην,   ἐκρύφθης,   ἐκρύφθη,
   ἐκρυφθήτην,   ἐκρυφθήτην,
   ἐκρύφθημεν,   ἐκρύφθητε,   ἐκρύφθησαν, the word.

6. Agrees with its Nominative Case (e. g. οἱ ἄνδρες) in Number and Person. Rule " Verbum Personale," &c.

Ex. 2. To parse the verb δέξασθαι.

1. δέξασθαι is a Verb from δέχομαι—Middle Form—Infinitive Mood—First Aorist Tense.

2. δέχομαι is a Verb in ω, Deponent, of the Second Conjugation (Characteristics, κ, γ, χ, σσ, ττ,) δέξομαι—δέδεγμαι —ἐδέχθην.

3. " Aoristum Primum Medium," &c. (§ 57, Gr. Gr.)

4. ἐδεξάμην, δέξαι, δέξωμαι, δεξαίμην, δέξασθαι, δεξάμενος, δέξασθαι, the word.

5. Infinitive (e. g.) preceded by a Nominative " Infinitivus Nominativum antecedentem capit," &c. (§ 162.)

Ex. 3. To parse the Verb βεβίασται.

1. βεβίασται is a Verb from βιάζομαι—Passive Form—Indicative Mood—Perfect Tense—Singular Number—Third Person.

2. Βιάζομαι is a Verb in ω, Deponent, of the Third Conjugation (Characteristics, τ, δ, θ, ζ)—βιάσομαι—βεβίασμαι —ἐβιάσθην.

3. " Perfectum Passivum Formatur," &c. (§ 61, Gr. Gr.)

4. βεβίασμαι, ἐβεβιάσμην, βεβίασο, βεβιασμένος ὦ, βεβιασμένος εἴην, βεβιάσθαι, βεβιασμένος.

5. βεβίασμαι,   βεβίασαι,   βεβίασται, the word.

6. Agrees with its Nominative Case (e. g. ὁ Κυρος) in Number and Person. Rule " Verbum Personale," &c.

Ex. 4. To parse the Verb ἐδηλοῦσθε.

1. ἐδηλοῦσθε is a Verb from δηλόω—Passive Voice—Indicative Mood—Imperfect Tense—Plural Number—Second Person.

2. δηλόω is a Verb of the Fifth Conjugation, (Characteristics all Vowels, and Diphthongs,) a Contract of the Third Formation—δηλώσω—δεδήλωκα—δεδήλωμαι—ἐδηλώθην.

3. "Imperfectum Medium et Passivum," &c. (§ 53, Gr. Gr.)

4. ἐδηλοόμην ἐδηλούμην,   δηλόου δηλοῦ,
   δηλόωμαι δηλῶμαι,   δηλοόιμην δηλοίμην,
   δηλόεσθαι δηλοῦσθαι,   δηλοόμενος δηλούμενος.

5. ἐδηλοόμην ἐδηλούμην,   ἐδηλόου ἐδηλοῦ,
   ἐδηλόετο ἐδηλοῦτο,   ἐδηλοόμεθον ἐδηλούμεθον,
   ἐδηλοέσθην ἐδηλούσθην,   ἐδηλοέσθην ἐδηλούσθην,
   ἐδηλοόμεθα ἐδηλούμεθα,   ἐδηλόεσθε ἐδηλοῦσθε, the word.

6. Agrees with its Nominative Case ὑμεῖς in Number and Person. Rule " Verbum Personale," &c.

§ 2. Verbs in μι.

1. Say from what Verb it comes—Voice (if one of the Deponents in § 79, Gr. Gr. say whether of the Passive or Middle Form) Mood—Tense—Number—Person.

2. Describe the Verb, stating to which of the four Formations of Verbs in μι it belongs. Give the Root, and if it be of the Fourth Formation, repeat the Obs. in p. 86, Gr. Gr. " Omnia ferè verba "—Principal Tenses, as in verbs in ω.

3. Give the Rules for the Formation of Verbs in μι, and for the two kinds of Reduplication. Then say the Rule for the Tense of the Verb parsed.

4. Cognate Tenses.

5. Go through the Tense until you come to the word.

6. State the Agreement or Government of the Verb, and give the Rule in either case.

4

Ex. 1. To parse the Verb δῶτε.

1. δῶτε is a Verb from δίδωμι—Active Voice—Subjunctive Mood—Second Aorist Tense— Plural Number—Second Person.

2. δίδωμι is a Verb in μι of the Third Formation—Root * δόω—δώσω—δέδωκα—δέδομαι—ἐδόθην.

3. Rules (p. 86, Gr. Gr.) " Verba in μι fiunt," &c. and "Reduplicatio duplex est," &c.—also the Rule, (p. 96) " Aoristum Secundum Activum," &c.

4. ἔδων, δὸς, δῶ, δοίην, δοῦναι, δούς.

5. δῶ,　　δῷς,　　δῷ,
δῶτον,　　δῶτον,
δῶμεν,　　δῶτε, the word.

6. Agrees with its Nominative Case ὑμεῖς in Number and Person. Rule " Verbum Personale," &c.

Ex. 2. To parse the Verb ἐδύναντο.

1. ἐδύναντο is a Verb from δύναμαι—Middle Form—Indicative Mood—Imperfect Tense—Plural.Number—Third Person.

2. δύναμαι is a Verb in μι, Deponent, of the First Formation—Root * δυνάω—δυνήσομαι—δεδύνημαι—ἐδυνήθην.

3. Rules, as in Ex. 1, for the Formation of Verbs in μι, and Rule (p. 96) for the Formation of the Imperfect Middle.

4. ἐδυνάμην, δύνασο, δυνῶμαι, δυναίμην, δύνασθαι, δυνάμενος·

5. ἐδυνάμην,　　ἐδύνασο,　　ἐδύνατο,
ἐδυνάμεθον,　　ἐδυνάσθην,　　ἐδυνάσθην,
ἐδυνάμεθα,　　ἐδύνασθε,　　ἐδύναντο, the word.

Agrees with its Nominative Case (e. g. οἱ Ἕλληνες) in Number and Person. " Verbum Personale," &c.

Ex. 3. To parse the Verb ἐσβέσθη.

1. ἐσβέσθη is a Verb from σβέννυμι—Passive Voice—Indicative Mood—First Aorist Tense—Singular Number—Third Person.

5

2. σβέννυμι is a Verb in μι of the Fourth Formation —Root * σβέω—"Omnia ferè verba quartæ formationis," &c. (p. 86, Gr. Gr.) σβέσω— ἔσβηκα, (p. 61)—ἔσβεσμαι— ἐσβέσθην.

3. Rules, as in Ex. 1, for the Formation of Verbs in μι, and the Rule (p. 81, § 64) for the First Aorist Passive of Verbs in ω.

4. ἐσβέσθην, σβέσθητι, σβεσθῶ, σβεσθείην, σβεσθῆναι, σβεσθείς.

5. ἐσβέσθην, ἐσβέσθης, ἐσβέσθη, the word.

6. Agrees with its Nominative Case (e. g. τὸ πῦρ) in Number and Person. " Verbum Personale," &c.

II. *Form of Parsing Defective and Anomalous Verbs.*

1. Say from what Verb it comes—Voice (if Deponent, whether of the Passive or Middle Form)—Mood—Tense— Number—Person.

2. Describe the Verb as Defective or Anomalous ; and if it be the latter, state to which Class of Anomalous Verbs it belongs, and give the Rule for the Class. If Defective, give the Rule and the Roots that supply its Tenses from p. 102, § 82 ; and if Anomalous, give the Root and Tenses in use from the " Synopsis Alphabetica " in § 93. Should it further be a Verb that *suffers Metathesis*, § 84, say so here, and shew how the transposition of letters takes place.

3. Rule for Formation of the Tense.

4. Cognate Tenses.

5. Go through the Tense until you come to the word.

6. State the Agreement or Government of the Verb, and give the Rule in either case.

EXAMPLES.

Ex. 1. To parse the Verb λάβωμεν.

1. λάβωμεν is a Verb from λαμβάνω—Active Voice— Subjunctive Mood—Second Aorist Tense—Plural Number— First Person.

2. λαμβάνω is an Anomalous Verb of the Fifth Class, Rule (p. 107, § 90) " Verba quæ præter literas," &c. Root *λάβω or λήβω. Second Aorist ἔλαβον, Future λήψομαι, Perfect Active εἴληφα, Perfect Passive εἴλημμαι and λέλημμαι, First Aorist Passive ἐλήφθην.

3. " Aoristum Secundum Activum," &c. (p. 82, § 66)

4. ἔλαβον, λάβε, λάβω, λάβοιμι, λαβεῖν, λαβών.

5. λάβω, λάβης, λάβη,
λάβητον, λάβητον,
λάβωμεν, the word.

6. Agrees with its Nominative Case ἡμεῖς in Number and Person. " Verbum Personale," &c.

Ex. 2. To parse the Verb ἐτέτμητο.

1. ἐτέτμητο is a Verb from τέμνω—Passive Voice—Indicative Mood—Pluperfect Tense—Singular Number—Third Person.

2. τέμνω is an Anomalous Verb of the Third Class, Rule (p. 106, § 88) " Verba quæ literam ν," &c. Root *τέμω, by Metathesis *τμέω, Future τεμῶ. Second Aorist ἔτεμον et ἔταμον, Perfect τέτμηκα, Perfect Passive τέτμημαι, First Aorist Passive ἐτμήθην.

3. " Pluperfectum Passivum Formatur," &c. (p. 81, § 62)

4. ἐτετμήμην, τέτμησο, τετμημένος ὦ, τετμημένος εἴην, τετμῆσθαι, τετμημένος.

5. ἐτετμήμην, ἐτέτμησο, ἐτέτμητο, the word.

6. Agrees with its Nominative Case (e. g. τὸ δένδρον) in Number and Person. " Verbum Personale," &c.

Ex. 3. To parse the Verb ἐνεχθήσεται.

1. ἐνεχθήσεται is a Verb from *ἐνέκω—Passive Voice—Indicative Mood—Future Tense—Singular Number—Third Person.

2. *ἐνέκω is an obsolete Root supplying the Tenses of the Defective Verb φέρω—Rule (p. 102) " Paucissima verba inveniuntur," &c.—φέρω, *οἴω, Fut. οἴσω—*ἔγκω, *ἐνέκω, *ἐνέγκω; First Aorist ἤνεγκα; Second Aorist ἤνεγκον, Per-

fect ἐνήνοχα, Perfect Passive ἐνήνεγμαι, First Aorist Passive ἠνέχθην, Future ἐνεχθήσομαι and οἰσθήσομαι. Verbal Adjectives οἰστός and φερτός.

3. "Futurum Primum Passivum," &c. (p. 81, § 65)

4. ἐνεχθήσομαι, ἐνεχθησόιμην, ἐνεχθήσεσθαι, ἐνεχθησόμενος.

5. ἐνεχθήσομαι, ἐνεχθήσει (or—ῃ), ἐνεχθήσεται, the word.

6. Agrees with its Nominative Case (e. g. τὸ βάρος) in Number and Person. "Verbum Personale," &c.

III. *Form of Parsing Participles.*

1. Say from what Verb it comes—Voice (if Deponent, say whether of the Passive or Middle Form)—Tense—Case —Number—Gender.

2. Describe the Verb according to the one of the foregoing Forms to which it belongs, giving the Root and Principal Tenses, if it be a regular Verb; and the Tenses in use, if Anomalous.

3. Rule for Formation of Tense.

4. Cognate Tenses.

5. Go through the Participle until you come to the word.

6. State the Substantive it agrees with, and the Rule for Agreement.

EXAMPLES.

Ex. 1. To parse λέξασαν.

1. λέξασαν is a Participle from the Verb λέγω—Active Voice—First Aorist Tense—Accusative Case—Singular Number—Feminine Gender.

2. λέγω is a Verb in ω of the Second Conjugation (Characteristics, κ, γ, χ, σσ, ττ,) λέξω—λέλεχα—λέλεγμαι —ἐλέχθην.

3. Aoristum Primum Activum," &c. (p. 76, § 57)

4. ἔλεξα, λέξον, λέξω, λέξαιμι, λέξαι, λέξας.

8

5. λέξας,   λέξασα,   λέξαν,
λέξαντος,   λεξάσης,   λέξαντος,
λέξαντι,   λεξάσῃ,   λέξαντι,
λέξαντα,   λέξασαν, the word.

6. Agrees with (e. g.) γύναικα in Case, Number, and Gender. Rule "Adjectiva participia et pronomina," &c. Second Concord in Latin Grammar, which is the same as in Greek. (§ 119)

Ex. 2. To parse θέντα.

1. θέντα is a Participle from the Verb τίθημι—Active Voice—Second Aorist Tense—Accusative Case—Singular Number—Masculine Gender.

2. τίθημι is a Verb in μι of the Second Formation—Root * θέω, θήσω, τέθεικα, τέθειμαι, ἐτέθην.

3. Rules (p. 86, Gr. Gr.) "Verba in μι fiunt," &c. and "Reduplicatio Duplex est"—also the Rule, (p. 96) "Aoristum Secundum Activum," &c.

4. ἔθην, θὲς, θῶ, θείην, θεῖναι, θείς.

5. θεὶς,   θεῖσα,   θέν,
θεντὸς,   θείσης,   θεντός,
θεντὶ,   θείσῃ,   θεντί,
θέντα, the word.

6. Agrees with (e. g.) τὸν Κῦρον in Case, Number and Gender. Rule as above for the Second Concord.

Ex. 3. To parse λαθούσαι.

1. λαθούσαι is a Participle from λανθάνω—Active Voice—Second Aorist Tense—Nominative Case—Plural Number—Feminine Gender.

2. λανθάνω is an Anomalous Verb of the Fifth Class—"Verba quæ præter literas," &c. (p. 107, § 90) Root * λάθω, λήθω. Second Aorist ἔλαθον, Future λήσω, Perfect Middle λέληθα, Perfect Passive λέλησμαι.

3. Rule p. 82, § 66, "Aoristum Secundum Activum," &c.

4. ἔλαθον, λάθε, λάθω, λάθοιμι, λαθεῖν, λαθών.

5. λαθών,   λαθοῦσα,   λαθόν,
λαθόντος,   λαθούσης,   λαθόντος,
λαθόντι,   λαθούσῃ,   λαθόντι,
λάθοντα,   λαθοῦσαν,   λαθόν,
λάθοντε,   λαθούσα,   λάθοντε,
λαθόντοιν,   λαθούσαιν,   λαθόντοιν,
λαθόντες,   λαθοῦσαι, the word.

6. Agrees (e. g.) with *αἱ κόραι*—in Case—Number—Gender. Rule as before for the Second Concord.

OBSERVATIONS.

1. If the Verb to be parsed be a separable Compound Verb, *i. e.*, if it be compounded with a Preposition, the Preposition must be separated from the Verb in the Section containing its description.

Thus (1) ἀπεκρύφθησαν is a Verb from ἀποκρύπτω—Passive Voice—Indicative Mood—First Aorist Tense—Plural Number—Third Person.

(2.) ἀποκρύπτω is a Verb compounded of the Preposition ἀπό and κρύπτω, which is a Verb of the First Conjugation, &c. and so on through (3) (4) and (5), at the end of which say—" ἐκρύφθησαν, adding ἀπό and eliding ο (by Rule in § 54, obs. 1, of Gr. Gr.) ἀπεκρύφθησαν, the word."

2. If it be an inseparable Compound, parse as a simple Verb, but give its Composition and Derivation at the end of the Form of Parsing.

Thus (1) ᾠκοδόμησαν is a Verb from οἰκοδομέω, &c. and so on, through (2) (3) (4) (5) and (6), at the close of which say, "οἰκοδομέω is a Verb compounded of οἶκος 'domus' and δέμω 'ædifico.'"

3. If it be a Dialectic Form state the fact at the commencement of the Form of Parsing, and give the Rule for it at the end.

Thus (1) ἔκρυφθεν is a Poetic Form for ἐκρύφθησαν—Passive Voice—Indicative Mood, &c. and so on in the Form prescribed; after (6) adding the Rule " Aoristi Passivi Tertia Persona Pluralis exit in εν pro ησαν." (p. 50, obs. 9)

c

4. Any Rule, at all bearing on the word parsed, may be required, in the same way, at the end of the Form.

5. In particular the Rules for the *Derivation* of Verbs (in p. 129, § 110), should be given here, where they are applicable.

IV. *Form of Parsing Nouns Substantive.*

1. Say from what the word comes—Case—Number—Gender.

2. Describe the Noun, stating to what Declension it belongs, and the Rule for the Declension.

3. Go through the Noun, until you come to the word.

4. Government, and Rule for Government.

N.B.—As in Parsing Verbs, the Composition and Derivation of the Noun should be given, where it can be ascertained, either from the Lexicon or the Rules for Derivation in Gr. Gr. (p. 102, § 102—105) The Rules also for any peculiarity of Dialect may be required, and, in Parsing Nouns of the Fifth Declension of Simples, the Rules for Formation of the *Cases* in pp. 15—17.

EXAMPLES.

Ex. 1. To parse the Noun Substantive κριταῖς.

1. κριταῖς is a Noun Substantive from κριτὴς—Dative Case—Plural Number—Masculine Gender.

2. κριτὴς belongs to the First Declension of Simples, whose terminations are ας and ης of the Masculine Gender. Rule " Prima Declinatio," &c. (p. 10, § 15)

3. κριτὴς,   κριτοῦ,   κριτῇ,   κριτὴν,   κριτὰ,
κριτα,   κριταῖν,
κριτὰι,   κριτῶν,   κριταῖς, the word.

4. Governed (e. g.) by the Verb ὠφελεῖ—Rule " Hinc quæ dandi, dicendi, auxiliandi," &c. (Gr. Gr. p. 175, § 134)

κριτὴς is a Verbal Noun, derived from the Verb κρίνω, denoting the Agent. Rule (p. 125, § 104) " Verbalia, quæ denotant agentem, desinunt in της," &c.

Ex. 2. To parse the Noun Substantive σοφίαν.

1. σοφίαν is a Noun Substantive from σοφία—Accusative Case—Singular Number—Feminine Gender.

2. σοφία belongs to the Second Declension of Simples, whose terminations are α and η of the Feminine Gender. It has a vowel before α, and therefore α is retained in all the Cases of the Singular. Rule " Secunda Declinatio," &c. (p. 11, § 16)

3. σοφία, σοφίας, σοφία, σοφίαν, the word.

4. Governed (e. g.) by the Transitive Verb ἐδίδαξε. Rule "Accusativus construitur," &c. (p. 177, § 138)

σοφία is derived from the Adjective σοφὸς, denoting an abstract quality. Rule "Substantiva derivata ab Adjectivis," &c. (p. 126, § 105)

Ex. 3. To parse the Noun Substantive κύνεσσι.

1. κύνεσσι is an Epic Form for κυσὶ, from the Noun Substantive κύων—Dative Case—Plural Number—Common Gender.

2. κύων belongs to the Fifth Declension of Simples, whose terminations are various, three, α, ι, υ, being of the Neuter Gender. " Quinta Declinatio," &c.

3. κύων, κυνὸς (by Syncope for κύονος, p. 16, obs. 6), κυνὶ, κύνε, κυνοῖν, κύνες, κυνῶν, κυσὶ, the word.

4. Governed (e. g.) by the Preposition σύν.

Rule " Epica lingua suum habet Dativum Pluralem " &c. (p. 17, § 24.) The Dative Plural is formed regularly from the Dative Singular, by inserting σ before the final ι, and casting away δ, θ, ν, τ, wherever they precede. Rule " Dativus Pluralis formatur," &c. (p. 17, § 24)

V. *Form of Parsing Nouns Adjective.*

1. Say from what the word comes—Case—Number—Gender.

2. Describe it, stating to which of the three Classes of Adjectives it belongs (p. 22, § 30), and to which Division of its Class according to the termination.

3. If it be in the Comparative or Superlative degree, give the Rule for forming degrees of comparison from § 33.

4. Go through the Adjective, until you come to the word.

5. Say with what Noun it agrees, and give the Rule for the Second Concord, which (see p. 165) is the same as that in the Latin Grammar (§ 136). Also, if it governs a Case, give the Rule of Government from the Syntax.

N.B.—As in Parsing Nouns, here give the Rule for Derivation and for any Dialectic or other peculiarity.

EXAMPLES.

Ex. 1. To parse the Noun Adjective χαρίεσσαν.

1. χαρίεσσαν is a Noun Adjective from χαρίεις—Accusative Case—Singular Number—Feminine Gender.

2. χαρίεις belongs to the First Class of Adjectives, having three terminations, and to division (b) of this Class. Rule "Adjectiva in tres Classes," &c. (p. 22)

4. χαρίεις,   χαρίεσσα,   χαρίεν,
χαρίεντος,   χαριέσσης,   χαρίεντος,
χαρίεντι,   χαριέσση,   χαρίεντι,
χαρίεντα,   χαρίεσσαν, the word.

5. It agrees (e. g.) with νύμφην in Gender, Number and Case. Rule "Adjectiva, participia," &c. χαρίεις is derived from the Substantive χάρις, the termination εις being one of those that denote *possession* or *property*. (p. 127, § 106)

Ex. 2. To parse the Noun Adjective εὐκλέα.

1. εὐκλέα is a Noun Adjective from εὐκλέης—Accusative Case—Singular Number—Masculine Gender.

2. εὐκλέης belongs to the Second Class of Adjectives, having two terminations, and to division (b) of this Class. Rule "Adjectiva in tres Classes," &c. (p. 22)

4. εὐκλέης   ῆς,   εὐκλέες εἶς,
εὐκλέεος   έους   οῦς,
εὐκλέεϊ   εὐκλέει   εῖ,
εὐκλέεα   εὐκλεᾶ, the word,

Which, by Rule, (in p. 25, § 31) "Quæ desinunt in ης purum," &c. is changed into the Form εὐκλέα.

5. It agrees (e. g.) with πότμον in Gender, Number, and Case. Rule for Second Concord.

εὐκλέης is derived from εὖ " benè " and κλέος " gloria."

Ex. 3. To parse the Noun Adjective τλημονεστάτῃ.

1. τλημονεστάτη is a Noun Adjective from τλημονέστατος— Dative Case—Singular Number—Feminine Gender.

2. τλημονέστατος belongs to the First Class of Adjectives, having three terminations, and to division (a) of this Class. Rule as above, " Adjectiva in tres Classes," &c. (p. 22)

3. It is in the Superlative Degree of Comparison, from the Positive τλήμων, formed by taking ον the termination of the Neuter, and inserting ες before τατος. (p. 28, (d))

4. τλημονέστατος,   -η,   - ον,
   τλημονεστάτου,   -ης,   -ου,
   τλημονεστάτῳ,   -ῃ, the word.

5. Agrees (e. g.) with γύναικι, in Gender, Number and Case. Rule for Second Concord.

τλήμων is derived from the Verb τλάω " fero."

VI. *Form of Parsing Pronouns.*

1. Say from what the word comes—Case—Number—Gender. If it be a Dialectic Form, state it here.

2. Describe the Pronoun as either Substantive or Adjective ; if the former, say whether it is a Personal, Reflexive, or Reciprocal Pronoun ; if the latter, whether Possessive, Relative, Indefinite or Demonstrative.

3. Go through it until you come to the word.

4. State the Agreement or Government, giving the Rule in either case.

14

Ex. 1. To parse the Pronoun ἡμᾶς.

1. ἡμᾶς is a Pronoun from ἐγὼ—Accusative Case—Plural Number—Masculine Gender (or Feminine, according to the context).

2. ἐγὼ is a Substantive Personal Pronoun of the First Person.

3. ἐγὼ, ἐμοῦ, ἐμοὶ, ἐμὲ, νὼ, νῶν, ἡμεῖς, ἡμῶν, ἡμῖν, ἡμᾶς, the word.

4. Governed by (e. g.) the Transitive Verb ἠγάπησεν. Rule " Accusativus Construitur," &c. (p. 117, § 138)

Ex. 2. To parse the Pronoun ᾗσι.

1. ᾗσι is an Ionic Form for αἷς, which is a Pronoun from ὃς " qui "—Dative Case—Plural Number—Feminine Gender.

2. ὃς is an Adjective Relative Pronoun, (p. 34 (b)).

3. ὃς, ἥ, ὃ; ου, ἧς, ου; ᾧ, ῃ, ᾧ; ὃν, ἥν, ὃ; ᾧ, ᾶ, ᾧ; οἵν, αἵν, οἵν; οἱ, αἱ, ᾶ; ὧν, ὧν, ὧν; οἷς, αἷς, the word.

4. Agrees with its Antecedent (e. g.) πολέων in Gender, Number and Person. Rule for Third Concord, as in Latin Grammar, § 137. " Relativum cum antecedente," &c.

Ex. 3. To parse the Pronoun ἕθεν.

1. ἕθεν is an Epic Form for ου " sui "—Genitive Case— Singular Number—Masculine Gender (or Feminine, according to the context).

2. οὗ is a Substantive Pronoun, partly Personal (of the Third Person), and partly Reflexive (say Rule in p. 32, obs. " Tertia Persona caret suo Pronomine," &c.)

3. (Go through the whole Pronoun)—οὗ, οἷ, ἓ; σφωΐν; σφεῖς, σφῶν, σφίσι, σφᾶς.

4. Governed (e. g.) by ἄξιος. Rule (p. 170, § 132) "Genitivus Construitur cum Verbis," &c.

N.B.—The other Dialects for οὗ are ἕο, εὗ Epic and Ionic, εἷο, ἑεῖο Epic, and ἑοῦς Æolic and Doric.

VII. *Form of Parsing Adverbs.*

1. Describe the Adverb—stating whether it is an Adverb of Place—Time—Manner—Quantity, &c.; also the Case (if any) which it governs, and the Rule of Government from the Syntax.

2. If it be of the Comparative or Superlative Degree, compare it, and give the Rule for Comparison, from § 97 of Gr. Gr.

3. As in Parsing Verbs, &c. here give the Rule for Derivation, and for any Dialectic or other peculiarity.

EXAMPLES.

Ex. 1. To parse the Adverb ἀξίως.

1. ἀξίως is an Adverb of Manner, governing the Genitive Case (e. g. λόγου). Rule "Genitivus construitur," &c. (§ 132)

3. ἀξίως is formed from the Adjective ἄξιος. Rule " Adverbia Modum Significantia," &c. (§ 112)

Ex. 2. To parse the Adverb ἥδιστα.

1. ἥδιστα is an Adverb of Manner, of the Superlative Degree.

2. ἡδέως, ἥδιον, ἥδιστα.

3. It is formed from the Adjective ἡδύς. (Rule as above from § 112)

Ex. 3. To parse οἴκοθεν.

1. οἴκοθεν is an Adverb of Place, signifying motion from a place. Rule (§ 113) "Adverbia Locum Significantia," &c.

2. It is derived from the Noun Substantive οἶκος "a house."

VIII. *Form of Parsing Prepositions.*

1. Describe the Preposition—stating to what Class it belongs, and give its general meaning. Mention the Case (or Cases) it governs, and the Prepositions of the same Class that govern the same Case (or Cases). If used Adverbially, say so.

2. If it has any peculiar force, different from the general meaning, find it in the List of Prepositions [in Part IV.] and quote the Example there given.

3. Rule as above for any peculiarity.

EXAMPLES.

Ex. 1. To parse the Preposition παρὰ, (e. g.) in the Sentence ἦλθον παρὰ τοῦ βασιλέως.

1. παρὰ is a Preposition of the Third Class, having the general meaning of "beside." It governs three Cases (Rule "Reliquæ sex ternos," &c. § 95) the Genitive, Dative and Accusative. It here governs the Genitive βασιλέως. The other Prepositions of the same Class are ἀμφὶ, ἐπὶ, περὶ, πρὸς and ὑπό.

Ex. 2. To parse the Preposition ἀφ', (e. g.) in the Sentence ἀφ' ἡμετέρας γνώμης.

1. ἀφ' is used for ἀπὸ, by elision of ο, and change of π into φ, before an aspirated Vowel. It is a Preposition of the First Class, having the general meaning "from" Lat. 'ab,' which is derived from ἀπό. It governs only the Genitive Case (Rule " Octo casum unum," &c.) as γνώμης in this Sentence. The other Prepositions of the same Division of the First Class are ἀντί, ἐκ or ἐξ, and πρό.

2. It has here the peculiar force of " at variance with " as in the phrases ἀπὸ δόξης, ἀπὸ θυμοῦ. [Part IV. 2 (d)]

3. Rule for elision "Elisio per Apostrophum," &c. (§ 8)

Ex. 3. To parse the Preposition ἐν, in the Sentence ἐν δὲ καὶ Λεσβίους εἷλε.

1. ἐν is a Preposition of the First Class, having the general meaning " in." It governs only the Dative Case. (Rule " Octo casum unum," &c.) The other Preposition of the same Division of the First Class is ξύν. It is here used adverbially by Rule (§ 180) " Præpositiones interdum tanquam adverbia usurpantur, imprimis ἐν et πρός."

IX. *Form of Parsing Conjunctions.*

1. Describe the Conjunction—saying whether it is Final—non-Final—Copulative—Disjunctive—or Partitive.

2. State the Mood to which it is joined, if it be either of the two former; and the Cases, Moods and Tenses it connects or disjoins, if it be either of the three latter. Give the Rule.

3. Give the Rule for any peculiarity.

EXAMPLES.

Ex. 1. To parse ἵνα (e. g.) in the sentence ταῦτα ἔγραφον ἵν' ἔλθοις.

1. ἵνα is a Final Conjunction.

2. It is here joined to the Optative Mood ἔλθοις, because used of a past thing. Rule (§ 155) " Finalis oratio," &c.

Ex. 2. To parse ὅτι (e. g.) in the sentence ' ἔλεγεν ὅτι κῦρος τεθνήκοι.'

1. ὅτι is a non-Final Conjunction referring to a *fact.*

2. It is here joined to the Optative Mood τεθνήκοι, because in *obliqua oratio.* Rule (§ 177 (a)) " Quæ ad factum," &c. and (§ 156) " Obliqua oratio, precedente Verbo," &c.

Ex. 3. To parse ἐὰν (e. g.) in the sentence ἐὰν (or ἢν) τοῦτο λέγῃς.

1. ἐὰν is a non-Final Conjunction, conditional.

2. It is here joined to the Subjunctive Mood λέγῃς, denoting Probability. Rule (§ 154 (b))

Ex. 4. To parse καὶ (e. g.) in the sentence δίκαιος καὶ σοφός.

1. καὶ is a Copulative Conjunction.

2. It here joins together the Nominative Cases δίκαιος and σοφός. Rule "Conjunctiones Copulativæ," &c. (Lat. Gr. § 167)

D

WORDS FOR PARSING.

I. *Regular Verbs.*

§ 1. Verbs in ω.

1. ἐτύψαμεν .... τύπτω .... strike.
2. λέξαι .... λέγω .... speak.
3. ἐτετυπείτην ...... τύπτω .... strike.
4. πλέξαιο .... πλέκω .... weave.
5. πεπλέχθαι .... πλέκω .... ———
6. πιθεῖν .... πείθω .... persuade.
7. σπεροῦμεν .... σπείρω .... sow.
8. ἔσπαρται .... σπείρω .... ———
9. βεβρεγμένοι ὦσι .... βρέχω .... moisten.
10. ἐνενεμήκεσαν ...... νέμω .... distribute.
11. ἐσπορέναι .... σπείρω .... sow.
12. παυθῶμεν .... παύω .... cause to cease.
13. λελέξεσθαι .... λέγω .... speak.
14. κέκοπται .... κόπτω .... beat.
15. ἐδοξάσθημεν ...... δοξάζω .... glorify.
16. σφαλεῖτε .... σφάλλω ...... deceive.
17. ἐκόψω ...., ... κόπτω .... beat.
18. δράξειας .... δράσσω .... grasp.
19. σφαγῶσι .... σφάττω .... slay.
20. αἰκισθῶσι .... ἀικίζω .... treat injuriously.
21. ὠνείδισε .... ὀνειδίζω .... reproach.

19

22. ψηφιεῖται ....ψηφίζω ....vote.
23. ἠναγκάσθη........ἀναγκάζω ......compel.
24. ἀπαλλάξαιμι......ἀπαλλάσσω ....set free.
25. ὡμολόγησαν ......ὁμολογέω ......confess.
26. ἐφίλεις ....φιλέω ....love.
27. ἐδηλοῦτε ....δηλόω ....shew.
28. δηλοῦσθαι ....δηλόω ....——
29. δηλοῖς (Subjunc.) ..δηλόω ....——
30. τιμᾶν............τιμάω ....honour.
31. ἐκάλει ....καλέω ....call.
32. ἐφοβεῖτο ....φοβέω ....frighten.
33. ποιήσῃς ....ποιέω ....do.
34. ἠπάτημαι ....ἀπατάω ....deceive.
35. νικῷεν ....νικάω..........conquer.
36. χρυσούτω ....χρυσόω ....gild.
37. ἐφιλείτην ....φιλέω..........love.
38. ἠλγοῦμεν ....ἀλγέω ....be in pain.
39. ἠσκεῖτε ....ἀσκέω ....exercise.
40. λελυπηκέναι ......λυπέω ....vex.
41. μισεῖν ....μισέω ....hate.
42. ἠκριβοῦτε ....ἀκριβόω........make exact.
43. ἐπλήρου ....πληρόω ....fulfil.
44. ἐπληροῦ ....πληρόω ....——
45. πληροῦ ....πληρόω ....——
46. ἀπατᾶσθαι........ἀπατάω ....deceive.
47. θεώμεθα..........θεάομαι ....behold.
48. νικηφορεῖ ..`......νικηφορέω ......carry off as a prize.
49. ἀνεσπάρασσον ....ἀνασπαράσσω ..tear up.
50. ἐπεκέλευσεν ......ἐπικελεύω ......exhort.
51. διέφυγον ....διαφεύγω ......escape.
52. προύβάλομεν ......προβάλλω ......put forward.

20

53. συνελέγετε .... συλλέγω .... collect.
54. περιέβαλες .... τεριβάλλω ...... throw around.
55. ἀμφεκαλύφθη ...... ἀμφικαλύπτω .... cover around.
56. διαφθεῖραι .... διαφθείρω ...... destroy.
57. διαλεχθῆναι ...... διαλέγομαι ...... converse.
58. ἐξέλαμψε .... ἐκλάμπω ...... shine forth.
59. συμβουλεύσαιμι .... συμβουλεύω .... advise.
60. συγχωρεῖν .... συγχωρέω ...... concede.
61. ἐισηγεῖσθαι ...... ἐισηγέομαι ...... introduce.
62. παρηγγέλθαι ...... παραγγέλλω .... send word.
63. ὑπέστρεψαν ...... ὑποστρέφω ...... return.
64. ἐισηγάγομεν ...... εἰσάγω .... lead in.
65. ἐισεπέμψατε ...... εἰσπέμπω ...... send in.
66. κατεσκεύασται .... κατασκευάζω .... prepare.
67. ἀπεθαύμασε ...... ἀποθαυμάζω .... admire.
68. ἀπῄτει .... ἀπαιτέω' .... demand back.
69. ἐξεθρέψαμεν ...... ἐκτρέφω .... rear up.
70. ἀπέφηνε .... ἀποφαίνω ...... declare.
71. ἐπετείχισαν ...... ἐπιτειχίζω ...... fortify.
72. μεταπέμψαι ...... μεταπέμπω .... send for.
73. παράγειν .... παράγω .... lead along.
74. παρετήρει .... παρατηρέω ...... observe.
75. προετίμησαν ...... προτιμάω ...... honour before.
76. προσεκαλοῦμεν .... προσκαλέω ...... summon.
77. κατέγραψαν ...... καταγράφω .... describe.
78. ὑπήκουσαν .. .. ὑπακούω .... listen to.
79. διεμνημόνευεν ...... διαμνημονεύω .... call to mind.
80. ἐπανορθώσασθαι .... ἐπανορθόω ...... set upright.
81. ἐπονομάζομεν ...... ἐπονομάζω ...... surname.
82. ἐξεργάζεται ...... ἐξεργάζομαι .... effect.
83. διαπράξασθαι ...... διαπράττω ...... accomplish.

21

84. παρεσκευάσθαι ....παρασκευάζω ....prepare.
85. καταγελᾶν ......καταγελάω ....laugh at.
86. ἀποβλέψαι ......ἀποβλέπω ......gaze at.
87. νενόμισται ....νομίζω ....own as a custom.
88. κατέλυσεν ....καταλύω ......destroy.
89. ἄρξαι ....ἄρχω ....begin.
90. πρόσταξον ....προστάσσω ....order.
91. διακωλύωσι ......διακωλύω ......hinder.
92. χαρίσασθαι ......χαρίζομαι ......gratify.
93. χαριεῖσθαι ....χαρίζομαι ......———
94. ἐξαπατηθείη ......ἐξαπατάω ....deceive thoroughly.
95. δεδηλωκέναι ......δηλόω ....shew.
96. ἐμποιῆσαι'........ἐμποιέω ....make in.
97. καρπώσασθαι......καρπόω ....bear fruit.
98. προστέτακται......προστάσσω ....order.
99. ἀναπληρῶσαι......ἀναπληρόω ....fill up.
100. ἐκφεύξεσθαι ....ἐκφεύγω ......escape.

§ 2. Verbs in μι.

1. ἱστάτην ....Ἵστημι ....make to stand.
2. ἱστᾶσι ....Ἵστημι ....———
3. δῶσι ....δίδωμι ....give.
4. δοῖεν ....δίδωμι ....———
5. δότε ....δίδωμι ....———
6. δόντων (Imperative) δίδωμι ....———
7. θῆτε ....τίθημι ....place.
8. θέτε ....τίθημι ....———
9. τιθεῖεν ....τίθημι ....———
10. τιθεῖσι............τίθημι ....———
11. δῶ ....δίδωμι ....give.
12. στῶμαι ....Ἵστημι ....make to stand.

13. στάσθαι .... ἴστημι .... make to stand.

14. ἰστῶμαι .... ἴστημι .... ————

15. θῇ (Active) ...... τίθημι .... place.

16. θῇ (Middle) ...... τίθημι .... ——

17. δοθείη .... δίδωμι .... give.

18. δόσθαι .... δίδωμι .... ——

19. θήσομαι .... τίθημι .... place.

20. ἔθηκαν .... τίθημι .... ——

21. δέδοται .... δίδωμι .... give.

22. ἔζευξαν .... ζεύγνυμι ...... join

23. μέμικται .... μίγνυμι ...... mingle.

24. ἐρράγη .... ῥήγνυμι ...... break.

25. ὀμωμοκέναι .... ὄμνυμι .... swear.

26. σβέσον .... σβέννυμι ...... extinguish.

27. ἐστρώμεθα .... στορέννυμι .... spread.

28. ἀπέδωκαν .... ἀποδίδωμι .... give back.

29. παρεδόθη .... παραδίδωμι .... hand over.

30. ἐξέθεσαν .... ἐκτίθημι ...... expose.

31. ἠπίστατο .... ἐπίσταμαι .... know.

32. μάρνασθαι .... μάρναμαι .... fight.

33. ἐκίνυντο .... κίνυμαι ...... advance

34. ἔτλη .... τλῆμι .... endure.

35. προὐδόθη .... προδίδωμι .... betray.

36. ἐξεδείξαντο .... ἐκδείκνυμι .... shew forth.

37. ἀποδόσθαι .... ἀποδίδωμι .... give back.

38. ἐσβήκασι .... σβέννυμι ...... extinguish

39. ἠδυνήθης (§ 53-2) .. δύναμαι ...... be able.

40. ἐζώσατο .... ζώννυμι ...... gird.

41. ἔζωσται .... ζώννυμι ...... ——

42. ἐξέστη .... ἐξίστημι ...... put out of place.

43. καθέστατο .... καθίστημι .... establish.

44. μεθεστηκέναι ......μεθίστημι ....change.
45. ἐφειστηκέιτην ......ἐφίστημι ......set over.
46. ἐκστῆτε ....ἐξίστημι ......put out of place.
47. παραστῶ ....παρίστημι ....place by.
48. περίδου ....περιδίδωμι .. wager (in midd. voice.)
49. δοθήσοιντο ....δίδωμι ....give.
50. ἀναθεῖναι..........ἀνατίθημι ....set up.

II. Anomalous Verbs, Defectives, &c.

1. βάλοιμι ....βάλλω .. ...cast.
2. εῖλεν ....αἱρέω ....take.
3. ἠνέχθημεν ....φέρω ....bear.
4. δραμοῦνται ....τρέχω........run.
5. σχεῖν ....ἔχω ....have.
6. ἔλθοιμι ....ἔρχομαι ......come.
7. θρέξεται ....τρέχω ....run.
8. ἐῤῥήθη............φημὶ ....say.
9. εἶεν..............εἰμί..........am.
10. ἔστων.............εἰμί..........——
11. ἔσοιντο ....εἰμί..........——
12. ἴτε ....εἶμι..........will go.
13. ᾔεσαν ....εἶμι..........————
14. ἴωμεν ....εἶμι..........————
15. ἰέναι ....εἶμι..........————
16. ἐτμήθη ....τέμνω ....cut.
17. ἐπράθομεν ....πέρθω ....lay waste.
18. πεπτωκέναι........πίπτω ....fall.
19. θάνω ....θνήσκω........die.
20. βληθείτην ....βάλλω........cast.
21. ἐξεπέσομεν ....ἐκπίπτω ......fall out.

24

22. ἀπώλεσαν .... ἀπόλλυμι ...... destroy.
23. ἤσθετο .... αἰσθάνομαι .... perceive.
24. ἑάλω .... ἁλίσκομαι .... am taken.
25. ἁμαρτεῖν .... ἁμαρτάνω .... err.
26. ὑπέσχετο .... ὑπισχνέομαι .... promise.
27. ἑήνδανον (§ 53, 8) .. ἁνδάνω .... please.
28. ἄραρε (§ 68, 3) .... ἀραρίσκω ...... fit.
29. ἀκαχεῖν .... ἀχέω .... grieve.
30. ἀναβῆναι .... ἀναβαίνω ...... ascend.
31. παρεβάθη .... παραβαίνω .... transgress.
32. βεβηκέναι .... βαίνω .... go.
33. βεβλῆσθαι .... βάλλω .... cast.
34. μέμβλωκε .... βλώσκω ...... come.
35. ἔγημε .... γαμέω .... marry.
36. γέγονε .... γίγνομαι ...... am born.
37. γεγενῆσθαι .... γίγνομαι ...... ————
38. γνῶναι .... γιγνώσκω ...... know.
39. δέδασται .... δαίω .... divide.
40. δέδηκται .... δάκνω .... bite.
41. διδάξαι .... διδάσκω ...... teach.
42. δέδοκται .... δοκέω .... seem.
43. δῦναι .... δύω .... go under.
44. ἀπήλασε .... ἀπελαύνω .... drive away.
45. ἐλαθῆναι .... ἐλαύνω ...... drive.
46. εὑρεῖν .... εὑρίσκω ...... find.
47. εὑρήκοιμι .... εὑρίσκω ...... ———
48. σχεθῆναι .... ἔχω .... have.
49. ἀφῖκται .... ἀφικνέομαι .... arrive.
50. ἵκμενος............ ἱκνέομαι ...... come.
51. κάμοιμι .... κάμνω ...... labour.
52. κεκμηκέναι .... κάμνω ...... ————

53. κιχεῖν .... κιχάνω ...... reach
54. κεκλαῦσθαι .... κλαίω... .... weep.
55. προσκυνῆσαι .... προσκυνέω .... salute.
56. λάχω .... λαγχάνω .... obtain by lot.
57. εἰλήχω............ λαγχάνω .... —————
58. λήξεσθαι .... λαγχάνω .... —————
59. λαβὲ .... λαμβάνω .... receive.
60. ἔλαβε .... λαμβάνω .... ———
61. λαβεῖν............ λαμβάνω .... ———
62. λήψωμαι .... λαμβάνω .... ———
63. εἴληφθον .... λαμβάνω .... ———
64. λάθω .... λανθάνω ...... lie hid.
65. λήσειν .... λανθάνω ...... ———
66. μαθήσεται .... μανθάνω ...... learn.
67. ἐμαχεσάσθην ..... μάχομαι .... fight.
68. ἐμνήσθητε.......... μιμνήσκω .... call to mind.
69. παρεμνήσω .... παραμιμνήσκω mention besides.
70. ὀλισθεῖν .... ὀλισθαίνω .... slip.
71. ἀπώλετο .... ἀπόλλυμι .... destroy.
72. ὀλούμεθα .... ὄλλυμι ...... ———
73. πάθω .... πάσχω ...... suffer.
74. πεπονθέναι .... πάσχω ...... ———
75. πείσεσθαι .... πάσχω ...... ———
76. πτέσθαι............ πέτομαι ...... fly.
77. πίοιμι .... πίνω .... drink.
78. καταπιεῖν .... καταπίνω .... swallow.
79. πέπωκε .... πίνω .... drink.
80. ποθῆναι ...., ... πίνω .... ———
81. πεπρᾶσθαι.......... πιπράσκω .... sell.
82. πυθώμεθα .... πυνθάνομαι .. enquire.

E

83. πέπυσται .... πυνθάνομαι .. enquire.
84. τεμεῖν .... τέμνω ...... cut.·
85. ταμεῖν .... τέμνω ...... ——
86. τετίχοιμι .... τίνω .... pay a price.
87. τετρώμεθα .... τιτρώσκω .... wound.
88. τευξόμεθα .... τυγχάνω .... obtain.
89. τύχοιμεν .... τυγχάνω .... ——
90. φθάσαι .... φθάνω ...... prevent.
91. χαρῆναι .... χαίρω ...... rejoice.
92. χραισμεῖν .... χραισμέω .... help.
93. ὤσασθαι .... ὠθέω .... thrust.
94. διαιρεθῆναι .... διαιρέω ...... divide.
95. ἐπιλάβοιο .... ἐπιλαμβάνω .. lay hold of.
96. ἐμβαλεῖν .... ἐμβάλλω .... cast in.
97. ἀπώσεις .... ἀπωθέω ...... thrust away.
98. ξυνθάνοιμεν .... ξυνθνήσκω .... die with.
99. ἀποφθίσαι .... ἀποφθίνω .... perish utterly.
100. πρόυδιδάξατο .... προδιδάσκω .. teach before.

III. *Participles (Miscellaneous.)*

1. τύπτουσι .... τύπτω ...... strike.
2. τυψάντων .... τύπτω ...... ——
3. πεπλεγμένων ...... πλέκω ...... weave.
4. φιλοῦντες .... φιλέω ...... love.
5. κινηθέντων .... κινέω .... move.
6. δόντων .... δίδωμι ...... give.
7. στάντι .... ἵστημι ...... make to stand.
8. θεῖσαις .... τίθημι ...... place.
9. δεδειγμένοις .... δείκνυμι ...... shew.

10. πεισάσῃ .... πείθω .... persuade.
11. βλαφθεῖσι .... βλάπτω ...... hurt.
12. παυσομένοις .... παύω .... cause to cease.
13. πεπεικυίαις .... πείθω .... persuade.
14. καμόντες .... κάμνω ...... labour.
15. διψῶντας .... διψάω ...... thirst.
16. ἐρωτωμένοις .... ἐρωτάω ...... ask.
17. νικηθέντες .... νικάω .... conquer.
18. ἠριθμημέναις .... ἀριθμέω ...... number.
19. ὁρμήσαντες .. .. ὁρμάω .... set in motion.
20. ζητούσης .... ζητέω .... seek.
21. κινουμένοις .... κινέω .... move.
22. μαρτυρούντων ...... μαρτυρέω .... bear witness.
23. αἰσθομένων .... αἰσθάνομαι .. perceive.
24. σχόντων .... ἔχω .... have.
25. λαχούσαις .... λαγχάνω .... obtain by lot.
26. προσβαλόντες ...... προσβάλλω .. add to.
27. ἐστερημένην .... στερέω ...... deprive.
28. φανέντα............ φαίνω ...... shew.
29. μαθούσαις .... μανθάνω .... learn.
30. ἐξολωλότος .... ἐξόλλυμι .... destroy utterly.
31. κείμενον............ κεῖμαι ...... lie down.
32. προσδεδεγμένη ...... προσδέχομαι .. accept.
33. ἐκπεπληγμέναις...... ἐκπλήσσω .... astonish.
34. ταρβήσασι.......... ταρβέω ...... dread.
35. ἀπελάσαντες .... ἀπελαύνω .... drive away.
36. ἀνασχομένων........ ἀνέχω ...... hold up.
37. ἀπολυθεῖσαι .... ἀπολύω ...... set free.
38. μεταβάντος .... μεταβαίνω .. depart.
39. ἀκολουθοῦντος ...... ἀκολουθέω .... follow.
40. μεμελετηκυῖαι ...... μελετάω .... practice.

41. προτετιμηκότας ......προτιμάω ....honour before.
42. δοξάζουσαν..........δοξάξω ......glorify.
43. ἀπηλλαγμένους ......ἀπαλλάσσω .. withdraw.
44. δράμοντα (Accus.) .. τρέχω ......run.
45. ἐντεταμένου .. ..ἐντείνω ......stretch.
46. ἀπολέσασαι ....ἀπόλλυμι ....destroy.
47. τελευτῶντα ....τελευτάω ....die.
48. ἐρωτώμενοι ....ἐρωτάω ......ask.
49. ἀναγεγραμμένῳ ....ἀναγράφω....write up.
50. κατειληφυίαις ......καταλαμβάνω seize upon.

IV. *Dialectic Forms.*

§ 1. Ionic Dialect.

1. τύπτεαι (§ 43.1) ....τύπτω ......strike.
2. ἐτύπτεο (§ 43.2) ....τύπτω ......————
3. ἐλέξαο (§ 43.2) ....λέγω........speak.
4. φιλέαι (§ 43.2) ....φιλέω ......love.
5. ἐκέατο (§ 43.4) ....κεῖμαι ......lie down.
6. ἐτυπτέατο (§ 43.4) .. τύπτω ......strike.
7. πυνθανοίατο (§ 43.4) πυνθάνομαι .. enquire.
8. βεβλάφαται (§ 43.8) βλάπτω......hurt.
9. πεπείθαται (§ 43.8).. πείθω........persuade.
10. κεκοσμέαται (§ 43.8) κοσμέω ......adorn.
11. νικηθέωσι (§ 43.11) νικάω........conquer.
12. λέγῃσι (§ 42.7) ....λέγω........speak.
13. ἐδέξαο (§ 43.2) ....δέχομαι......receive.
14. ζητέαι (§ 43.2)......ζητέω ......seek.
15. ἐσκευάδατο (§ 43.8) .. σκευάζω ....prepare.
16. ἐλελέχατο (§ 43.8) .. λέγω........speak.

17. βλαφθέης (§ 43.11) .. βλάπτω ...... hurt.
18. χρέωνται (§ 44.2) .. χράομαι .... use.
19. ἐφίλευν (§ 44.3) .... φιλέω .... love.
20. ἀποχρεωμένων (§ 44.2) ἀποχράομαι .. am contented with.
21. φοιτέοντα (§ 44.2) .. φοιτάω ...... roam about.
22. φοβέο (§ 44.3) .... φοβέω ...... terrify.
23. μισεύμεθα (§ 44.3) .. μισέω .... hate.
24. στεφανεῦνται (§ 44.4) στεφανόω .... crown.
25. ἰδρῴην (§ 44.5) .... ἰδρόω .... sweat.
26. συνεπεπτώκεε (§ 4.2) συμπίπτω .... fall together.
27. ἀπίκετο (§ 4.2) .... ἀφικνέομαι .... arrive.
28. ἐνορῴη (§ 43.p. 53) .. ἐνοράω ...... see in.
29. ἐσπέμπεσκον (§ 53.10) εἰσπέμπω .... send in.
30. ἐδικαίευ (§ 44.4) .... δικαιόω ...... justify.
31. ἀσπάζοντο (§ 53.9) .. ἀσπάζω ...... salute.
32. ἔοργεε (§ 4.2) .... ῥέζω .... do.
33. ἀμείβετο (§ 53.9) .. ἀμείβομαι .... answer.
34. παρέχοντο (§ 53.9) .. παρέχω ...... offer.
35. δόσκομεν (§ 72.5) .. δίδωμι .... give.
36. στέωμεν (§ 72.9) .. ἵστημι .... cause to stand.
37. κατεστεῶτα (§ 81(b)) καθίστημι .... establish.
38. δώωσι (§ 72.9) .... δίδωμι .... give.
39. δύνεαι (§ 73.1) .... δύναμαι ...... am able.
40. παρετιθέατο (§ 73.2) παρατίθημι .... place by.
41. ἔνθεο (§ 73.3) .... ἐντίθημι ...... place in.
42. προσθέοιτο (§ 73.5) .. προστίθημι .... add to.
43. ἔσαν (§ 80) ...... εἰμί .... am.
44. ἔσκε (§ 80) .... εἰμί .... —
45. ἔμεναι (§ 80) ...... εἰμί .... —
46. ἤϊε (§ 80) .... εἶμι .... will go.
47. λάμψεται (§ 93) .. λαμβάνω ...... receive.

30

48. βώσαντες (p. 137)..βοάω ....cry out.
49. ἐπιβώσασθαι (p.137) ἐπιβοάω ......call upon.
50. προηδέατο (§ 43.4)..προαιδέομαι ....owe one honour.
51. ἀπαιρήσεαι (p. 137) ⎫
    and § 43.1) ....⎬ἀφαιρέομαι ....take away.
52. ἀπεθώυμαζε (p. 137) ἀποθαυμάζω....wonder at.

§ 2. Doric Dialect.

1. δεδοίκαμες (§ 42.1⎫
   and § 58.1) ....⎬δείδω..........fear.

2. τεθνάκαμες (§ 42.1⎫
   and p. 136) ....⎬θνήσκω ....die.

3. ἤνθομες (§ 42.1, and⎫
   p. 136)........⎬ἔρχομαι ....come.

4. ἐψιθυρίσδομες(§42.1⎫
   and p. 136)....⎬ψιθυρίζω........whisper.

5. λαλεῦμες (§ 42.1⎫
   and § 44.3) ....⎬λαλέω ....speak.

6. ὀισεῦμες (§ 42.1,⎫
   § 44.3, and§ 55.5)⎬φέρω ....bear.

7. σταξεῦμες (§ 42.1 ;⎫
   § 44.3 ; and § 47.⎬στάζω..........drop.
   (c) 1) ....⎭

8. βᾶμες (§ 42.1, p.⎫
   136 and § 53.9)..⎬βαίνω ....go.

9. μοχθίσδοντι (§ 42.1⎫
   and p. 136) ....⎬μοχθίζω ....toil.

10. ᾠδήκαντι (§ 42.1⎫
    and p. 136) ....⎬οἰδαίνω ....swell.

11. βομβεῦντι (§ 42.1⎫
    and § 44.3) ....⎬βομβέω ....buzz.

12. σιγῶντι (§ 42.1) ..σιγάω..........am silent.

13. χρήσδοντι (§ 42.1⎫
    and p. 136) ....⎬χρήζω ....desire.

31

14. ναίοισι (§ 42.1) ....ναίω ....dwell.

15. τύρισδες (§ 42.2 ;
p. 136, and § 53.9)} συρίζω ....pipe.

16. διδάκκη (§ 42.2)....διδάσκω ....teach.

17. πεπόνθης (§ 42.2) ..πάσχω ....suffer.

18. κτείνησθα (§ 42.6)..κτείνω ....kill.

19. νίπτητι (§ 42.7) ....νίπτω ....wash.

20. κοσμῆν (§ 44.3)....κοσμέω ....adorn.

21. λάσεμεν (§ 42.12 and
p. 136)........} λανθάνω ....lie hid.

22. ἁρμόσεν (§ 42.12)..ἁρμόζω ....adapt.

23. κατενθῆν (§ 42.12
and p. 136)....} κατέρχομαι......come to.

24. εἰπῆν (§ 42.12) ....ἔπω ....speak.

25. ῥέξαις (§ 42.13)....ῥέζω ....do.

26. ῥίψαισα (§ 42.13)..ῥίπτω ....throw.

27. ποθορῆ (§ 44.2)....προσοράω ....look at.

28. ὅρη (Imper. § 44.2) ὁράω............see.

29. ἐγέλαξε (§ 47.4 (e)) γελάω ....laugh.

30. ὠθεῦνται (§ 44.3).. ὠθέω ....thrust.

31. βιάσδευ (p. 136 and
§ 44.3)........} βιάζομαι........use violence.

32. κινησεῖται (§ 56.1)..κινέω ....move.

33. λάμπεσκον (§ 53.10) λάμπω ....shine.

34. ἐρητύσασκε (§ 53.10) ἐρητύω ....restrain.

35. φυλαξεῖς (§ 55.5) ..φυλάσσω ....guard.

36. φθεγξεῖται (§ 56.1) φθέγγομαι ......speak.

37. νομευσῶ (§ 55.5) ..νομεύω..........pasture.

38. ἀσεῦμαι (§ 56.1 and
§ 44.3)........} ἀδω............sing.

39. πευσεῖσθε (§ 56.1) ..πυνθάνομαι ......enquire.

40. τίθητι (§ 72.3) ....τίθημι ....place.

32

41. φατί (for φησί. § 72.3)
    and p. 136) .... } φημί ....speak.

42. ἴστ αντι (§ 72.3)....ἴστημι ....place.

43. ἐντί (for ἐστί, § 80)..εἰμί ....am.

44. λαψῆ (§ 93) ......λαμβάνω ....receive.

45. ἔφθαξα (§ 93) ....φθάνω ....prevent.

46. βασεῦμαι (§ 56.1)
    and p. 136) .... } βαίνω ....go.

47. φράσδεο (§ 43.2, and
    p. 136) ....} φράζομαι ....consider.

48. ἀραξεῖ (§ 55.5) ....ἀράσσω ....beat.

49. χαίροισα (p. 136) ..χαίρω ....rejoice.

50. βωκολιαξῆ (1 Fut.)
    Med. § 56.1 and } βουκολιάζω ......write pastorals.
    p. 136)........)

§ 3. Æolic Dialect.

1. λέξεις (Att. § 42.11) λέγω ....speak.

2. φροντίσειαν (§ 42.11) φροντίζω ....reflect.

3. ἀλλάξειας (§ 42.11) ἀλλάσσω........exchange.

4. κρύψειαν (§ 42.11)..κρύπτω.........conceal.

5. στείλεις (§ 42.11) ..στέλλω ....set in order.

6. φήνειας (§ 42.11) ..φαίνω ....shew.

7. δουλεύσειαν (§ 42.11) δουλεύω ....enslave.

8. παιδεύσειεν (§ 42.11) παιδεύω ....instruct.

9. ἀγαπᾶμες (§ 44.2) ἀγαπάω ....love.

10. δαπανᾶμες (§ 44.2) δαπανάω ....spend.

11. τολμᾶμες (§ 44.2) τολμάω ....endure.

12. ἐρωτᾶντι (§ 44.2) ..ἐρωτάω ....ask.,

13. διψᾶντι (§ 44.2) ..διψάω ....thirst.

14. τολμᾶντι (§ 44.2) ..τολμάω ....dare.

15. περεβάλομεν (§ 54.1) περιβάλλω ......cast around.

16. πεπάγασι (*Dor.* p. 136) .... } πήγνυμι .... fix.

17. κίρναις (*Dor.* p. 136) .. κίρνημι .... mingle.

18. φωνοίσας for φωνούσης (*Dor*.p. 136) .... } φωνέω .... call.

19. μοχθήσειαν (§ 42.11) ∴ μοχθέω .... labour.

20. κολυμβᾶμες (§ 44.2).. κολυμβάω ...... swim.

§ 4. Epic or Homeric Dialect.

1. κτείνωμι (§ 42.5) .... κτείνω .... kill.

2. ἐρύσσομεν for ἐρύσωμεν (§ 42.8) .... } ἔρυω .... draw.

3. ἐλαυνέμεναι (§ 42.12) .. ἐλαύνω .... drive.

4. φράζεαι (§ 43.1) ...... φράζω .... speak.

5. ἐπιτέλλεο (§ 43.2) .... ἐπιτέλλω ...... order.

6. μεταφρασόμεσθα (§ 43.2) ...... } μεταφράζω .... translate.

7. εἰρύαται (§ 43.4) .... ἐρύω .... draw.

8. ἐφθίατο (§ 43.4) .... φθίνω .... pine.

9. ἐβήσετο (§ 43.6) .... βαίνω .... go.

10. ἤγερθεν (§ 43.9) .... ἐγείρω .... raise up.

11. φάανθεν (§ 43.9) .... φαίνω .... show.

12. ὁμοιωθήμεναι (§ 43.13) ὁμοιόω .... compare.

13. ὁρόων (§ 44.2) ...... ὁράω .... see.

14. ἀντιόωσαν (§ 44.2) .. ἀντιάω .... meet.

15. φορήμεναι (§ 44.3) .. φορεῖν .... bear.

16. ἀρόωσι (§ 44.4) .... ἀρόω .... plough.

17. ἐλέλιξεν (§ 47 (c) 1).. ἐλελίζω .... shake.

18. κρήηνον (§ 57.1) .... κραίνω .... accomplish.

19. δέχθαι (62 obs.) .... δέχομαι .... receive.

20. πεπίθοιντο (66.3) .... πείθω .... persuade.

F

34

34

21. ἔσταν (72.7) .... ἴστημι ...... place.
22. ξύνιεν (§ 72.7) ...... ξυνίημι .... understand.
23. ἀνέσταν (§ 72.7) .... ἀνίστημι ...... raise up.
24. σύνθεο (§ 73.3) ...... συντίθημι ...... set together.
25. μεθέμεν (§ 72.13) .... μεθίημι .... set loose.
26. μάρναο (§ 73.3) .... μάρναμαι ...... fight.
27. δόμεναι (§ 72.13) .... δίδωμι .... give.
28. δώωσι (§ 72.9) .... δίδωμι .... ——
29. ἐνικάτθεο (§ 73.3) .... ἐγκατατίθημι .. lay in.
30. θέμεν (§ 72.13) .... τίθημι .... place.
31. ζώεσκον (§ 53.10) .... ζάω .... live.
32. ποθέεσκεν (§ 53.10) .. ποθέω .... regret.
33. κεχαροίατο (§ 43.4)
    and § 66.3) .... } χαίρω .... rejoice.
34. ὑπόσχεο (§ 43.2) .... ὑπισχνέομαι .... promise.
35. κάββαλε (for κατέβαλε).. καταβάλλω cast down.
36. τετάρπετο (§ 66.3) .. τέρπω .... delight.
37. τετύχοιμι (§ 66.3) .. τυγχάνω ...... obtain.
38. ἐιλήλουθμεν (§ 82) .. ἔρχομαι ...... come.
39. ἤγρετο (§ 83) ...... ἐγείρω .... raise up.
40. ἐκέκλετο (§ 83) .... κέλομαι .... exhort.

§ 5. Nouns Substantive.

1. δεσπόταις .... δεσπότης ...... master.
2. ὑποκριτῶν .... ὑποκριτής ...... actor.
3. θάλασσαν .... θάλασσα ...... sea.
4. νύμφας .... νύμφη .... nymph.
5. ἡδοναῖν .... ἡδονή .... pleasure.
6. ἀνδρείᾳ .... ἀνδρεία .... manliness.
7. ἰατροῖς .... ἰατρός .... physician.
8. καιρῶν .... καιρός .... time.

9. δήμῳ............δῆμος..........people.
10. ὀστᾶ............ὀστέον........bone.
11. νήσοις ....νῆσος..........island.
12. φαρμάκοις........φάρμακον......drug.
13. δώρων ....δῶρον..........gift.
14. ψηφίσμασι ......ψήφισμα ......vote.
15. κυμάτων ....κῦμα..........wave.
16. δράκουσι ....δράκων........serpent.
17. ἀκτῖσι ....ἀκτίν ....ray.
18. ποιμένας ....ποιμήν ....shepherd.
19. θῆρες ....θήρ ....wild beast.
20. μάρτυρας ....μάρτυρ........witness.
21. ἐλέφασι..........ἐλέφας ....elephant.
22. ὄρνιθας ....ὄρνις ....bird.
23. λαμπάδων........λαμπάς ....torch.
24. χάριτες ....χάρις ....favour.
25. τείχη............τεῖχος ....wall.
26. μέλεσι ....μέλος ....limb.
27. πρᾶξιν ....πρᾶξις ....action.
28. πρεσβέων ....πρέσβυς ......old man.
29. φονεῦσι ....φονεύς ....murderer.
30. ἠχοῖ ....ἠχώ ....echo.

§ 6. Nouns Adjective.

1. τυφλοῖς ....τυφλός ....blind.
2. δήλους ....δῆλος..........manifest.
3. χαλεπῶν ....χαλεπός ......hard.
4. λυγραῖν..........λυγρός ....mournful.
5. δημοσίᾳ..........δημόσιος ......public.
6. ἐχθραῖς ....ἐχθρός ....hostile.
7. ψυχρὰν ....ψυχρός ....cold.

8. ἱμερόεσσαν........ἱμερόεις........lovely.

9. πτερόεντα (Plur.)..πτερόεις......winged.

10. φωνήεσσαις......φωνήεις........vocal.

11. ῥοδόεσι.........ῥοδόεις........rosy.

12. βαθὺν...........βαθύς........deep.

13. γλυκεῖαν........γλυκύς........sweet.

14. ἡδέσι............ἡδύς..........——

15. θρασέων.........θρασύς........bold.

16. ὠκείαις.........ὠκύς.........swift.

17. θανασίμοιν........θανάσιμος......deadly.

18. ἐρήμοις.........ἔρημος........desert.

19. ἀγλαῶν.........ἀγλαός........splendid.

20. ἀληθέσι.........ἀληθής........true.

21. ἀκριβέων.......ἀκριβής........accurate.

22. δημώδεας.......δημώδης......popular.

23. πετρώδεα.......πετρώδης......rocky.

24. ψευδείαις.......ψευδής........false.

25. ἀμύμονες.......ἀμύμων........blameless.

26. ἐλεήμοσι.......ἐλεήμων......pitiful.

27. εὐδαίμονας......εὐδαίμων......happy.

28. οἰκτιρμόνων......οἰκτίρμων......compassionate.

29. τλημόνοιν.......τλήμων........patient.

30. μνήμονε.........μνήμων........mindful.

§ 7. Miscellaneous Dialectic Forms of Nouns Substantive and Adjective, and Pronouns.

1. παγαῖσι (Dor. p. 136 and § 12 obs.)....} πηγή......fountain.

2. μώσας (Dor. p. 136)....μοῦσα....song.

3. ἐπέεσσι (Ep. § 24.2)..ἔπος......word.

4. ἀνθερίκεσσι (Ep. § 24.2)..........} ἀνθέριξ....ear of corn.

5. ὄρχως (*Dor.* § 18.4) .. ὄρχος ....orchard.

6. βώκολον(*Dor.* p. 136) .. βούκολος ..herdsman.

7. σκολιῆσι (*Ion.* § 15.2) .. σκολιός ....crooked.

8. ὡρᾶν (*Dor.* p. 136) ....ὡρὰ........season.

9. φρασὶν (for φρεσὶν,
   Dor. p. 136)......} φρὴν ......mind.

10. θέμιστας (*Ep.* § 22.4) .. θέμις ......justice.

11. ὡρανῶ (for οὐρανοῦ,
    Dor. p. 136)......} οὐρανὸς ....heaven.

12. φιλότατα(*Dor.* p. 136) .. φιλότης ....friendship.

13. χαλεπᾶν(*Dor.* p. 136) .. χαλεπὸς ....hard.

14. μεριμνᾶν(*Dor.* p. 136) .. μεριμνή ....care.

15. κυλίκεσσι (*Ep.* § 24.2) .. κύλιξ......cup.

16. ὀππάτεσσι (*Ep.* and
    Æol. § 24.2) ....} ὄμμα ......eye.

17. τῆνον (*Dor.* p. 136)....ἐκεῖνος......he.

18. ἀδεῖαν (*Dor.* p. 136)....ἡδὺς ......sweet.

19. μεσαμβρίην (*Ion.* p.
    137)............} μεσημβρία ..noon.

20. νήεσσι (*Ion.* § 20.1
    § 24.2 ....} ναῦς........ship.

21. νούσων (*Ion.* p. 137) ..νοῦσος ......disease.

22. θωύμασι(*Ion.* p. 137) ..θαῦμα ......wonder.

23. κιθῶνας(*Ion.* p. 137) ..χιτὼν ......garment.

24. γουνάτων (*Ion.* §.
    22.5) ....} γόνυ........knee.

25. ὄρεσφι (*Ep.* § 29.1) ..ὄρος ....mountain.

26. νεηνίην (*Ion.* § 16) ....νεανίας......young man.

27. τεῦς (*Æol.* § 37) ....σὺ..........thou.

28. σέθεν (*Poët.* § 37) ....σὺ.........——

29. ἄμμες (*Æol.* § 38) ..ἐγώ ....I.

30. ὑμμεών (*Æol.* § 38) ..σὺ.........thou.

38

PART II.

GREEK TREES.

IT has been thought desirable to give an example of a Greek Tree for each of the five Conjugations, in order to prevent the confusion often produced in a boy's mind, when he has to write Trees for the other Conjugations, with a model perhaps of the first only before him. He should open his Grammar at p. 70 (§ 53), and form the Tenses according to the Rules given in pp. 70—83. It will be found most convenient to enter the Tenses in the Tree, in the order of succession in which the Rules follow in the Grammar.

First Conjugation.

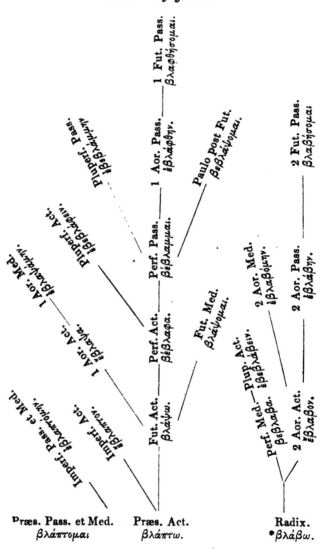

1 Fut. Pass.
βλαφθήσομαι.

Plusperf. Pass.
ἐβεβλάμμην.

1 Aor. Pass.
ἐβλάφθην.

Paulo post Fut.
βεβλάψομαι.

2 Fut. Pass.
βλαβήσομαι

Plusperf. Act.
ἐβεβλάφειν.

Perf. Pass.
βέβλαμμαι.

2 Aor. Med.
ἐβλαβόμην.

1 Aor. Med.
ἐβλαψάμην.

Perf. Act.
βέβλαφα.

Fut. Med.
βλάψομαι.

2 Aor. Pass.
ἐβλάβην.

1 Aor. Act.
ἔβλαψα.

Fut. Act.
βλάψω.

Perf. Med.—Plup. Act.
βέβλαβα. ἐβεβλάβειν.

Imperf. Act.
ἔβλαπτον.

2 Aor. Act.
ἔβλαβον.

Imperf. Pass. et Med.
ἐβλαπτόμην.

Præs. Pass. et Med.
βλάπτομαι

Præs. Act.
βλάπτω.

Radix.
*βλάβω.

Words for Greek Trees.

First Conjugation.

1. δρέπω........*δράπω ....pluck.
2. ἐρείπω ......*ἐρίπω............overthrow.
3. λείπω........*λίπω ....leave.
4. σήπω ....*σάπω............to cause to rot.
5. τέρπω........*τάρπω ....delight.
6. ἀμείβω ....change.
7. θλίβω ....bruise.
8. στείβω ......*στίβω ....tread.
9. τρίβω ....rub.
10. ἀλείφω ....anoint.
11. γλύφω ....carve.
12. γράφω ....write.
13. στέφω ....crown.
14. βάπτω ......*βάφω ....dip.
15. βλάπτω ......*βλάβω ....injure.
16. καλύπτω......„.*καλύβω..........hide.
17. κόπτω... ....*κόπω ....beat.
18. κρύπτω ......*κρύβω ....conceal.
19. νίπτω........*νίβω ....wash.
20. ῥάπτω........*ῥάφω ....sew.
21. ῥίπτω ....*ῥίφω ....cast.
22. σκάπτω ......*σκάφω ....dig.
23. σκολύπτω ....*σκολύφω,—βω ....tear up.
24. σκώπτω ......*σκώπω ....jest.
25. κολάπτω......*κολάφω..........buffet.

G

Second Conjugation.

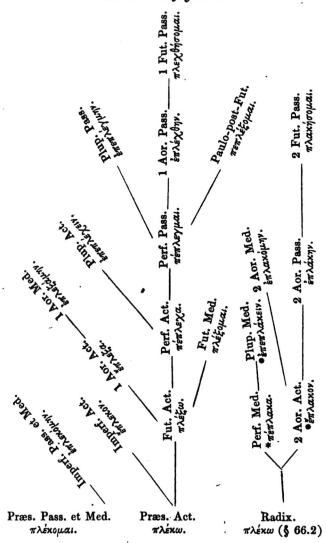

1 Fut. Pass. πλεχθήσομαι.

1 Aor. Pass. ἐπλέχθην.

Plup. Pass. ἐπεπλέγμην.

Paulo-post-Fut. πεπλέξομαι.

2 Fut. Pass. πλαχήσομαι.

Perf. Pass. πέπλεγμαι.

Plup. Act. ἐπεπλέχειν.

2 Aor. Med. ἐπλαχόμην.

2 Aor. Pass. ἐπλάχην.

Perf. Act. πέπλεχα.

Fut. Med. πλέξομαι.

Plup. Med. *ἐπεπλάχειν.

1 Aor. Med. ἐπλεξάμην.

1 Aor. Act. ἐπλέξα.

Fut. Act. πλέξω.

Perf. Med. *πέπλαχα.

2 Aor. Act. *ἔπλαχον.

Imperf. Act. ἔπλεκον.

Imperf. Pass. et Med. ἐπλεκόμην.

Præs. Pass. et Med. πλέκομαι.

Præs. Act. πλέκω.

Radix. πλέκω (§ 66.2)

Words for Greek Trees.

Second Conjugation.

1. διώκω ....pursue.
2. πλέκω ....*πλάκω..........weave.
3. ἄγω ....lead.
4. οἴγω ....open.
5. τρώγω ....*τράγω..........gnaw.
6. φεύγω ....*φύγω ....fly from.
7. ἀλλάσσω ......*ἀλλάγω ....change.
8. θωρήσσω ......*θωρήκω ....arm.
9. κηρύσσω ......*κηρύκω ....proclaim.
10. μαλάσσω ......*μαλάκω ....soften.
11. μάσσω ....*μάγω ....wipe off.
12. ὀρύσσω ....*ὀρύγω ....dig.
13. πατάσσω ......*πατάγω ....strike.
14. πλήσσω........*πλήγω ....——
15. πράσσω ......*πράγω ....act.
16. σπαράσσω.....................lacerate.
17. σταλάσσω......*σταλάγω ......drop.
18. σφάττω........*σφάγω ....slay.
19. ταράσσω ......*ταράχω ....disturb.
20. τάσσω ....*τάγω ....set in order.
21. ἄρχω ....rule.
22. ψύχω ....*ψύγω ....cool.
23. φλέγω ....burn.
24. πνίγω ....suffocate.
25. κορύσσω ....arm.

Third Conjugation.

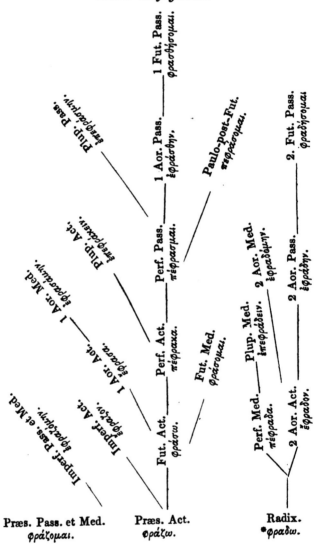

1 Fut. Pass. φρασθήσομαι.

1 Aor. Pass. ἐφράσθην.

Plup. Pass. ἐπεφράσμην.

Paulo-post-Fut. πεφράσομαι.

2. Fut. Pass. φραδήσομαι.

Perf. Pass. πέφρασμαι.

Plup. Act. ἐπεφράκειν.

2 Aor. Med. ἐφραδόμην.

2 Aor. Pass. ἐφράδην.

1 Aor. Med. ἐφρασάμην.

Perf. Act. πέφρακα.

Plup. Med. ἐπεφράδειν.

1 Aor. Act. ἔφρασα.

Fut. Med. φράσομαι.

Perf. Med. πέφραδα.

Imperf. Act. ἔφραζον.

Fut. Act. φράσω.

2 Aor. Act. ἔφραδον.

Imperf. Pass. et Med. ἐφραζόμην.

Præs. Pass. et Med. φράζομαι.

Præs. Act. φράζω.

Radix. *φραδω.

45

Words for Greek Trees.

Third Conjugation.

1. πείθω ....*πίθω............persuade.
2. πλήθω ....fill.
3. ἀναγκάζω ....compel.
4. ἁρπάζω.........*ἁρπάγω ....seize.
5. γυμνάζω ......*γυμνάδω ....exercise.
6. δοκιμάζω ....prove.
7. δοξάζω ....glorify.
8. ἑτοιμάζω ....prepare.
9. κλάζω ....*κλάγω ....clash.
10. κολάζω ....punish.
11. κράζω ....*κράγω...........cry out.
12. ὀνομάζω ....name.
13. πλάζω ....*πλάγχω ....cause to err.
14. σκευάζω ......*σκευάδω ....equip.
15. ἀικίζω ....ill-use.
16. κομίζω ....*κομίδω ....bear.
17. νομίζω ....think.
18. ὁπλίζω ....arm.
19. ὁρίζω...........................terminate.
20. στηρίζω ....*στηρίγω ....fix.
21. σχίζω ....*σχίδω...........cleave.
22. ὑβρίζω ....*ὑβρίδω ....insult.
23. ψηφίζω ....*ψηφίδω ....vote.
24. ἁρμόζω ....*ἁρμόδω ....adapt.
25. ἀθροίζω ....assemble.

Fourth Conjugation.

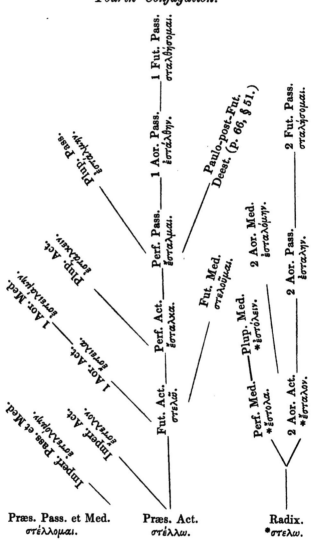

47

Words for Greek Trees.

Fourth Conjugation.

1. ἀγγέλλω .... bring news.
2. ποικίλλω .... variegate.
3. σφάλλω .... deceive.
4. νέμω .... distribute.
5. μένω .... remain.
6. εὐφραίνω .... cheer.
7. θερμαίνω .... warm.
8. ἰαίνω .... cheer.
9. κραίνω .... accomplish.
10. μαραίνω .... wither.
11. μιαίνω .... pollute.
12. περαίνω .... complete.
13. σημαίνω .... signify.
14. φαίνω .... shew.
15. κτείνω .... kill.
16. τείνω .... extend.
17. κλίνω .... incline.
18. κρίνω .... judge.
19. ἀμβλύνω .... blunt.
20. θαρσύνω .... encourage.
21. μηκύνω .... prolong.
22. μολύνω .... pollute.
23. ὀξύνω .... sharpen.
24. σπείρω .... sow.
25. φθείρω .... destroy.

Fifth Conjugation.

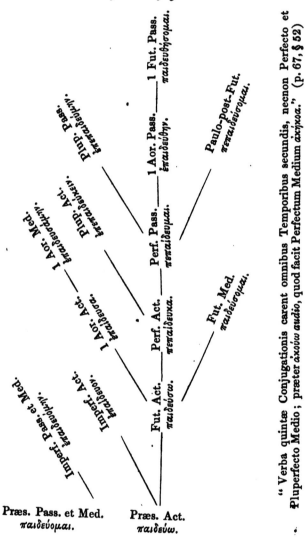

1 Fut. Pass. παιδευθήσομαι.

1 Aor. Pass. ἐπαιδεύθην.

Paulo-post-Fut. πεπαιδεύσομαι.

Plup. Pass. ἐπεπαιδεύμην.

Plup. Act. ἐπεπαιδεύκειν.

Perf. Pass. πεπαίδευμαι.

1 Aor. Med. ἐπαιδευσάμην.

1 Aor. Act. ἐπαίδευσα.

Perf. Act. πεπαίδευκα.

Fut. Med. παιδεύσομαι.

Fut. Act. παιδεύσω.

Imperf. Act. ἐπαίδευον.

Imperf. Pass. et Med. ἐπαιδευόμην.

Præs. Pass. et Med. παιδεύομαι.

Præs. Act. παιδεύω.

"Verba quintæ Conjugationis carent omnibus Temporibus secundis, necnon Perfecto et Pluperfecto Medio; præter ἀκούω audio, quod facit Perfectum Medium ἀκήκοα." (p. 67, § 52)

49

Words for Greek Trees.

Fifth Conjugation.

1. δουλεύω .... enslave.
2. κινδυνεύω .... endanger.
3. κωλύω .... hinder.
4. παύω .... make to cease.
5. φυτεύω .... plant.
6. ψαύω .... touch.
7. ἀπατάω .... deceive.
8. γεννάω .... beget.
9. ἐρωτάω .... ask.
10. ἡττάω .... overcome.
11. κοιμάω .... lull asleep.
12. νικάω .... conquer.
13. πειράω .... tempt.
14. ἀδικέω .... injure.
15. ἀσκέω .... exercise.
16. ζητέω .... seek.
17. κινέω .... move.
18. κοσμέω .... adorn.
19. λυπέω .... vex.
20. αἱματόω .... cover with blood.
21. δουλόω .... enslave.
22. ἐρημόω .... lay waste.
23. ζημιόω .... punish.
24. πληρόω .... fill.
25. στεφανόω .... crown.

H

PART

Irregular Greek Verbs

Present.—English.	Radical Form.	Future.	Perf. Active.	Perf. Passive.
αἱρέω......D. take	*ἕλω........	αἱρήσω......	ᾕρηκα .... ἀραίρηκα,Ion	ᾕρημαι...... ἀραίρημαι..Ion.
αἰσθάνομαι.... perceive	*αἴσθομαι....	αἰσθήσομαι ..	....	ᾔσθημαι......
ἁλίσκομαι ..D. am taken	*ἁλόω......	ἁλώσομαι	ἑάλωκα.... ἥλωκα	....
ἁμαρτάνω.... err	*ἁμάρτω....	ἁμαρτήσομαι..	ἡμάρτηκα..	....
ἀνδάνω...... please	*ἅδω........	ἁδήσω	....	....
ἀραρίσκω.... fit	*ἄρω........	ἄρσω........	....	ἀρήρεμαι ..Ep.
αὐξάνω...... increase	αὔξω	αὐξήσω......	ηὔξηκα....	ηὔξημαι, ηὔξησα
βαίνω ...... go	*βάω..with α lengthened	βήσομαι......	βέβηκα....	βέβαμαι ....
βάλλω....M. throw	*βάλω *βλάω lengthened	βαλῶ, βαλλήσω	βέβληκα ..	βέβλημαι .... βεβόλημαι, Ep.
βιβρώσκω.... eat	*βρόω ..with βι prefixed	....	βέβρωκα ..	βέβρωμαι···...
βλώσκω...... come	*μόλω..*βλόω	μολοῦμαι	μέμβλωκα	....
βούλομαι .... wish	....	βουλήσομαι ..	....	βεβούλημαι ..

N.B.—Words with *D*. prefixed are from the list of Defectives in Gr. Gr. (§ 82)

III.

of frequent occurrence.

First Aorists.	First Future Passive.	Second Aorists.	Second Perfect.	Remarks, &c.
ἠρέθην	αἱρεθήσομαι	εἷλον		
....	....	εἱλόμην		
....	....	ἠσθόμην		
....	....	ἑάλων ἥλων	....	supplies Passive Tenses of αἱρέω.
....	....	ἥμαρτον....	....	*Ep.* 2 *Aor.* ἤμβροτον.
....	....	εὔαδον, *Poet.* ἔαδον	ἔαδα	*Imperf.* ἥνδανον, ἑάνδανον, ἐήνδανον.
ἦρσα, ἤρθην....	....	ἤραρον	ἄραρα	2 *Aor. M. Part.* ἄρμενος.
ηὐξήθην	αὐξηθήσομαι	....	....	*Fut. Midd.* has a Passive meaning.
ἔβησα, ἐβάθην	....	ἔβην	βέβαα	Transitive in *Fut. Act.* and 1 *Aor. Act.*
ἐβάλλησα	βληθήσομαι	ἔβαλον		
ἐβλήθην......	....	ἔβλην .. *Ep.*		
ἐβρώθην......	....	ἔβρων .. *Ep.*	....	Other Tenses supplied by ἐσθίω, ἔδω, *φάγω (§ 82)
....	....	ἔμολον		
ἐβουλήθην	....	....	*In Compos.* προβέβουλα	N.B. — This Verb takes Augment η. (§ 53)

Those with *M.* prefixed are from the list of words that suffer Metathesis (§ 84)

52

Irregular Greek Verbs

Present.—English.	Radical Form.	Future.	Perf. Active.	Perf. Passive.
γαμέω .... marry, i.e. take a wife	*γάμω	γαμῶ	γεγάμηκα..	γεγάμημαι ..
γηράω γηράσκω grow old	....	γηράσομαι	γεγήρακα ..	....
γίγνομαι .... be, become	*γένομαι..with γι prefixed	....	....	γεγένημαι ....
γιγνώσκω .... γινώσκω know	*γνόω..with γι prefixed	γνώσομαι	ἔγνωκα	ἔγνωσμαι ....
δάκνω ...... bite	*δάκω	δήξομαι	δέδηχα	δέδηγμαι ....
δείδω .... fear	....	δείσομαι	δέδοικα .... δείδοικα, Ep.	:............
διδάσκω ...... teach	*δάω ..with δι prefixed	διδάξω	δεδίδαχα ..	δεδίδαγμαι....
δοκέω .... seem	*δόκω	δόξω .... δοκήσω ..Poet.	δεδόκηκα ..	δέδογμαι .... δεδόκημαι
ἐλαύνω ...... drive	*ἐλάω..with a lengthened	ἐλάσω, ἐλῶ ..	ἐλήλακα ..	ἐλήλαμαι ....
ἔρχομαι....D. go, come	*ἐλεύθω...... *ἐλύθω	ἐλεύσομαι	ἐλήλυθα .. εἰλήλουθαEp	....
ἐσθίω......D. eat	ἔδω ....Ep.	ἔδομαι ...... ἐδοῦμαι	ἐδήδοκα	ἐδήδεσμαι ....

of *frequent occurrence.*

First Aorists.	First Future Passive.	Second Aorists.	Second Perfect.	Remarks, &c.
ἔγημα ..... ἐγαμήθην	....	....	....	*Midd.* γαμοῦμαι, I am married—I take a husband.
ἐγήρασα.....	....	ἐγήραν	....	*Att. Infin. Aor.* γηρᾶναι.
ἐγενήθην......	γενηθήσομαι	ἐγενόμην ..	γέγονα	*Part. Ep.* γεγαώς.
ἐγνώσθην	γνωσθήσομαι	ἔγνων	γέγαα, Poet. οἶδα ..from *εἴδω	*Imperat.* γνῶθι.
ἐδήχθην	δηχθήσομαι.	ἔδακον	....	
ἔδεισα	....	....	δέδια......	*Imp.* δέδιθι.
ἐδίδαξα ..... ἐδιδάχθην	....	....	....	*Fut. Poet.* διδασκήσω.
ἔδοξα, ἐδόκησα ἐδόχθην	....	....	....	*Impers.* δοκεῖ, it seems, and δέδοκται, de-cretum est.
ἤλασα, ἠλάθην				
....	....	ἤλυθον	....	2 *Aor. Dor.* ἤνθον.
....	....	*Sync.* ἦλθον.	....	*Fut.* εἶμι and *Imperf.* ἤειν or ἦα are pre-ferred by the *Attics.*
ἠδέσθην	....	ἔφαγον	ἔδηδα	*Ep. Infin.* ἔδμεναι.
....	....	....	....	*Fut. M.* φάγομαι.

54

Irregular Greek Verbs

Present.—English.	Radical Form.	Future.	Perf. Active.	Perf. Passive.
εὑρίσκω find	*εὕρω	εὑρήσω	εὕρηκα	εὕρημαι
ἔχω ......D. have	*σχω	ἔξω or σχήσω	ἔσχηκα	ἔσχημαι
θνήσκω ....M. die	*θάνω *θνάω	θανοῦμαι	τέθνηκα	
ἵημι send	*ἕω	ἥσω	εἶκα	εἶμαι
ἱκνέομαι come	ἵκω ....Ep.	ἵξομαι		ἵγμαι
καλέω ....M. call	*κάλω *κλάω	καλέσω	κέκληκα	κέκλημαι
κάμνω ....M. grow weary	*κάμω *κμάω	καμοῦμαι	κέκμηκα	
λαγχάνω .... obtain by lot	*λάχω *λήχω	λήξομαι	εἴληχα, λέλογχα,Ion	εἴληγμαι
λαμβάνω .... receive	*λάβω *λήβω	λήψομαι λάμψομαι, Ion.	εἴληφα λελάβηκα	εἴλημμαι λέλημμαι λέλαμμαι
λανθάνω, λήθω escape notice	*λάθω	λήσω λασεῦμαι, Dor.		λέλησμαι λέλασμαι
μανθάνω .... learn	*μάθω *μήθω	μαθήσομαι μαθεῦμαι, Dor.	μεμάθηκα	

of frequent occurrence.

First Aorists.	First Future Passive.	Second Aorists.	Second Perfect.	Remarks, &c.
εὑρέθην	....	εὑρον, εὑρόμην		
ἐσχέθην	....	ἔσχον	....	*Imperf.* εῖχον.
		ἐσχόμην ..	....	*Dor. Imper.* σχές.
....	....	ἔθανον	....	*Infin. Perf.* τεθνάναι.
.........., ...	....	....	....	*Part.* τεθνεὼς,—ηώς.
ἦκα, ἕηκα .. *Ion.*				
ἔθην, εῖσα				
....	....	ἱκόμην		
ἐκάλεσα	κληθήσομαι	....	....	*P. p. Fut.* κεκλήσομαι
ἐκλήθην				
....	....	ἔκαμον		
ἐλήχθην	....	ἔλαχον	....	*Redupl.* 2 *Aor.*
				λέλαχον, *Fut. Ion.*
				λάξομαι.
ἔλαμψα .. *Ion.*				
ἐλήφθην	ληφθήσομαι	ἔλαβον		
ἐλάμφθην	....	λάβεσκον		
ἔλησα	....	ἔλαθον	λέληθα	*Redupl.* 2 *Aor.*
ἐλάσθην				λέλαθον.
....	....	ἔμαθον		

Present.—English.	Radical Form.	Future.	Perf. Active.	Perfect Passive.
μάχομαι .... fight — ἔομαι *Ep.* and *Ion.*	....	μαχοῦμαι .... —ἔσομαι	....	μεμάχημαι ..
μιμνήσκω .... remember	*μνάω ..with μι prefixed.	μνήσω	....	μέμνημαι ....
ὄλλυμι ...... destroy	*ὄλω (εω.) ..	ὀλῶ ...... *Att.* ὀλέσω .... *Ep.*	ὀλώλεκα ..	....
ὁράω ......D. see	supplied by *ὄπω *εἴδω.	ὄψομαι	ἑώρακα	ὤμμαι ...... ἑώραμαι
πάσχω ...... suffer, for πάθσκω	*πάθω *πένθω.	πείσομαι	....	....
πίνω .... drink	*πίω *πόω....	πίομαι	πέπωκα	πέπομαι ......
πυνθάνομαι .. learn by en- quiry	πεύθομαι, *Poet.*	πεύσομαι	....	πέπυσμαι ....
τέμνω ...... cut	*τέμω, *Metath.* *τμέω	τεμῶ	τέτμηκα ..	τέτμημαι ....
τίνω .... pay, suffer	*τίω	τίσω	τέτικα	τέτισμαι ....
τρέχω ....D. run	supplied by *δρέμω	δραμοῦμαι .... θρέξομαι..*rar.*	δεδράμηκα..	....

of frequent occurrence.

First Aorists.	First Future Passive.	Second Aorists.	Second Perfect.	Remarks, &c.
ἐμαχεσάμην				
ἔμνησα	μνησθήσομαι			μεμνήσομαι, *P. p. Fut.*
ἐμνήσθην				
ὤλεσα		ὠλόμην	ὄλωλα ..am undone	*Fut. Midd.* ὁλοῦμαι.
ὤφθην	ὀφθήσομαι	εἶδον, εἰδόμην	ὄπωπα. .*Ion.*	Takes double augment. 2 *Sing. Fut.* ὄψει.
		ἔπαθον	πέπονθα	πέποσθε 2 *Pl.* 2 *Pers.* for πεπόνθατε.
ἐπόθην	ποθήσομαι	ἔπιον		*Imper.* 2 *Aor.* πίε, πῖθι.
		ἐπυθόμην		*Ep. Optat.* πεπύθοιτο.
ἐτμήθην	τμηθήσομαι	ἔταμον ἔτεμον		*P. p. Fut.* τετμήσομαι
ἐτίσθην, ἔτισα..				The *Attics* have ι short, the *Epics* ι long, in all the Tenses.
ἔθρεξα ....*rar.*		ἔδραμον		

58

Irregular Greek Verbs

Present.—English.	Radical Form.	Future.	Perf. Active.	Perfect Passive.
τυγχάνω .... obtain, hap-pen, hit	τεύχω	τεύξομαι	τετύχηκα .. τέτευχα, Ion.	τέτυγμαι ....
φέρω ......D. bring	supplied by *οἴω *ἔγκω *ἐνέκω *ἐνέγκω	οἴσω	ἐνήνοχα ..	ἐνήνεγμαι ....
φθάνω ...... prevent, an-ticipate	*φθάω	φθήσομαι	ἔφθακα	
φθίνω φθίω.... decay, de-stroy	....	φθίσω (trans.) φθίσομαι (intrans)	....	ἔφθιμαι ......
χαίρω ...... rejoice	....	χαιρήσω	κεχάρηκα ..	κεχάρημαι .... κέχαρμαι ....
χανδάνω .... contain	*χάδω *χάνδω.	χείσομαι	κέχανδα ..	....
χέω .... pour	....	χέω......Att. χεύω ....Ep.	κέχυκα	κέχυμαι......
ὠθέω .... push	*ωθω	ὤσω and ὠθήσω.	ἔωκα	ἔωσμαι ......

of frequent occurrence.

First Aorists.	First Future Passive.	Second Aorists.	Second Perfect.	Remarks, &c.
ἐτεύχθην ἐτύχθην	....	ἔτυχον	....	3 *Pl. Perf. Pass.* τετεύχαται.
ἤνεγκα ...... ἠνέχθην	ἐνεχθήσομαι. οἰσθήσομαι	ἤνεγκον	....	*old Aor. Imper.* οἶσε.
ἔφθασα	....	ἔφθην	....	*Dor. Fut.* φθάξω. *Aor.* *Midd. Part.* φθάμενος.
ἔφθισα (*trans.*)	....	ἐφθίμην.... (*intrans.*)	....	like τίνω, has ι short in *Att.* long in *Ep.* writers.
χήρατο .. *Ep.* from ἐχηράμην	....	ἐχάρην	....	*Red.* 2 *Aor.* κεχα- ρόμην.
....	....	ἔχαδον		
ἔχεα, ἔχευα, *Ep* ἐχύθην ὦσα .. *Ep. Ion.* ἐώσθην	χυθήσομαι..	ἐχύμην	....	1 *Aor. Midd.* ἐχεάμην and ἐχευάμην, *Ep.* *Imperf.* ἐώθουν.

Cognate Tenses of a few Verbs of frequent occurrence.

	Imperative.	Subjunctive.	Optative.	Infinitive.	Participle.
ἔβην 2 Aor. (βαίνω)	βῆθι	βῶ	βαίην	βῆναι	βάς.
ἔτλην 2 Aor. (*τλάω)	τλῆθι		τλαίην	τλῆναι	τλάς.
ἑάλων 2 Aor. (ἁλίσκομαι) ..	ἁλῶθι ..	ἁλῶ	ἁλοίην	ἁλῶναι	ἁλούς.
ἔσχον 2 Aor. (ἔχω)	σχές	σχῶ	σχοίην	σχεῖν	σχών.
ἔγνων 2 Aor. (γιγνώσκω) ..	γνῶθι..	γνῶ	γνοίην	γνῶναι	γνούς.
ἔδυν 2 Aor. (δύνω)	δῦθι	δύω	δύην	δῦναι....	δύς.
οἶδα ἤδειν } P. M. (εἴδω)	ἴσθι	εἰδῶ	εἰδείην	εἰδέναι	εἰδώς.
εἰμί ἦν } sum	ἴσθι	ὦ	εἴην	εἶναι	ὤν.
εἶμι ᾔειν } ibo.	ἴθι	ἴω	ἴοιμι	ἰέναι	ἰών.

PART IV.

ON THE GREEK PREPOSITIONS.

THE original object of all Prepositions is the same—*viz.* to express the idea of *position* or *motion* in *space*. From this general meaning are derived, in various ways, the relations of *time*—*cause*—*effect,* &c.

There are eighteen Prepositions, which are divided into three Classes, according to the number of Cases they govern. The first Class contains those that govern only one Case. The second Class, those that govern two Cases. The third Class, those that govern three Cases.

I. *First Class.*

Prepositions governing only one Case.

The first Class contains eight Prepositions. Four of these, ἀντὶ, ἀπὸ, ἐκ (or ἐξ), πρὸ, govern a *Genitive* Case. Two, ἐν, σὺν (or ξύν), govern a *Dative* Case. Two, ἀνὰ, εἰς (or ἐς), with which ὡς *to* is related, govern an *Accusative* Case.

§ 1. Prepositions governing only a Genitive Case.

I. ἀντὶ.

The primary meaning of ἀντὶ is OVER AGAINST, OPPOSITE TO.

62

Derivative Significations.

a. **As good as, equal to** (Lat. *instar*)—ἀντὶ πολλῶν λαῶν ἐστί, *he is worth many people.*

b. **Instead of**—ἀντ' ἀγαπῆς μῖσος, *hatred instead of love.*

c. **In return for, equivalent to, in exchange for** —δύο ἀντὶ μιᾶς ψυχάς, *two lives for one.* So ἀνθ' ὧν, *wherefore.*

d. It is used after Comparatives, and by itself sometimes signifies Comparison, as in ἓν ἀνθ' ἑνός, *one set against the other.*

e. It is used also with Verbs of **entreaty** and **adjuration**; ἀντὶ παίδων τῶνδέ σε, πάτερ, ἱκετεύομεν, *we entreat thee, father, by these children.*

Significations in Composition.

a. **Opposition**—ἀντιλέγω, *to contradict.*

b. **Equality, balancing**—ἀντάξιος, *equivalent.*

c. **Reciprocation, requital**—ἀντωφελεῖν, *to benefit in turn.*

d. **Rivalry**—ἀντίτεχνος, *rivalling in a craft.*

II. ἀπό (Lat. *a* or *ab*.)

The primary meaning of ἀπὸ is FROM. It differs from ἐκ in that it signifies *from, away from*, generally, and when used of space, from the *exterior* of an object, whereas ἐκ denotes motion from the *interior—out of.* It differs from παρά, in being chiefly used of inanimate things, whereas παρά is almost always used of animate things.

DERIVATIVE SIGNIFICATIONS.

a. **Motion from a place**—ἄγειν ἀπ' ἀκτῆς, *to lead from the shore.*

b. **Distance** or **interval of space**—ἡ θάλασσα ἀπέχει ἀπὸ τῆς λίμνης ὡς τέσσαρα στάδια, *the sea is distant about four furlongs from the lake.*

c. **Distance** or **interval of time**—ἀφ' οὗ Σωκράτει συνδιατρίβω (sc. χρόνου), *since I have been living with Socrates.* Hence **after**, as γενέσθαι ἀπὸ δείπνου, *to finish dinner.*

d. **Separation from**, without the idea of motion— κεκρυμμένος ἀπ' ἄλλων, *hidden from the rest.* Hence the idea of **at variance with**— ἀπὸ δόξης, *contrary to one's opinion:* ἀπὸ θυμοῦ, *disagreeable.*

e. **Origin, descent, derivation, &c.**—φῦναι ἀπό τινος, *to be sprung from any one:* οἱ ἀπὸ Σπάρτης, *the Spartans.* οἱ ἀπὸ Πλάτωνος, *the Platonic School.*

f. The **instrument** of an action—πέφνεν ἀπ' ἀργυρέοιο βίοιο, *he slew them with a silver bow.*

g. The **moral source** of an action—ἀπ' ὀρθῆς γνώμης πάντα μοι πέπρακται, *I have done everything from an upright spirit:* ἀπὸ τῆς χαρᾶς (N. T.) *through joy.*

h. The **material** of which a thing is made—ἀπὸ ξύλου, *made of wood.*

SIGNIFICATIONS IN COMPOSITION.

a. **Separation**—as in ἀποβαίνειν, ἀποβάλλειν.

b. **Ceasing to be**—ἀπογίνεσθαι, *to die,* i.e. to be as it were *unborn* : ἀποστράτηγος, *an ex-general.*

64

c. **Completion**—ἀπέχουσι μισθὸν (N. T.) *they have their full reward.*

d. **Negation**—ἀπόφημι, *I deny* : ἀπειπεῖν ὁμιλίαν, *to re-nounce intercourse.*

e. It augments the force of words—ἀποδεικνύναι, *to prove thoroughly* : ἀποθαυμάζειν, *to admire excessively.*

PHRASES.

ἀπὸ γλώσσης, *by word of mouth.* ἀπὸ μνήμης, *by heart.* ἀπὸ τύχης, *by chance.* ἀπὸ τοῦ παραχρῆμα, *at once, suddenly.* ἀπὸ τοῦ ἀδοκήτου, *unexpectedly.*

III. ἐκ or ἐξ (Lat. *e. ex.*)

'Εκ is closely allied in meaning with ἀπὸ, and signifies FROM, with the additional idea of motion from the *interior* of a place or thing (See under ἀπὸ). Thus, ἐκ τῆς πόλεως φεύγειν, *to fly from within a city* : whereas ἀπὸ κ. τ. λ. would signify only that the person had been *near* the city. This distinction, however, is not always observed.

DERIVATIVE SIGNIFICATIONS.

a. It is used with Verbs implying *rest* as well as motion— καθήμεθ' ἄκρων ἐκ πάγων, *we sit on the heights* (and look down from them).

b. Like ἀπὸ it signifies a **space** or **interval of time**— ἐξ οὗ (sc. χρόνου) *since.* Hence simply **after**—γελᾶν ἐκ δακρύων, *to laugh after tears.* Cf. ἐκ θυσίας γενέσθαι, *to make an end of sacrificing.*

c. **Origin, birth, descent,** though implying a *nearer* relation than ἀπὸ, as (e. g.) between a son and father, ἐξ ἐμοῦ γένος ἐσσί, *thou art of my blood.*

d. **Cause, motive, impulse**—ἐκ θυμοῦ φιλεῖν, *to love from the heart* : ἐξ ἔριδος μάχεσθαι, *to fight from a feeling of hatred.*

e. **Material**—οὐκ ἐκ ξύλων ποιεῦνται τὰ πλοῖα, *they do not make their boats of wood.*

f. It is sometimes used for ὑπό—ἐφίληθεν ἐκ Διός, *they were beloved by Zeus* (chiefly in Herodotus.)

SIGNIFICATIONS IN COMPOSITION.

a. **Removal from,** as in ἐκβάλλειν, ἐκδιδόναι κ. τ. λ.

b. Like ἀπό, it **intends** or **augments,** and conveys the idea of *fully* accomplishing or carrying out, as in ἐξευρίσκειν : ἐκπολιορκοῦν, *to take a city by siege* : ἐξαιτέομαι, *I obtain by entreaty.*

PHRASES.

ἐκ (for ἔξω) βελέων, *out of shot.* ἐξ ἴσου, *equally.* ἐκ τοῦ ἐμφανοῦς, *openly.* ἐκ προαιρέσεως, *on purpose.* ἐκ βίας, *forcibly.* ἐξ ἑτοίμου, *promptly.*

IV. πρὸ.

The general meaning of πρὸ is BEFORE. It agrees with ἀντὶ in all its relations, but is used more extensively.

DERIVATIVE SIGNIFICATIONS.

a. **Before** in regard to **place**—πρὸ θυρῶν, *before the doors* : and with *persons,* as πρὸ τοῦ βασιλέως, *before the king.*

b. In regard to **time**—as πρὸ πολλῶν ἐτέων, *many years before* : πρὸ ὥρας, *prematurely.*

c. As the Latin *præ,* to express a **preference**—κέρδος πρὸ δίκης αἰνέσαι, *to praise craft before justice.* Thus, πρὸ πάντων ἂν ποιησαίμην, *I should choose before anything—I would give anything to——.*

d. **Substitution** and so **protection,** with the notion of standing *in front* of another and taking his place : μάχεσθαι πρὸ παίδων, *to fight for one's children.*

K

e. Some expressions seem to connect πρό with the Latin *porrò, forwards :* πρὸ ὁδοῦ, *further on the road,* whence the Attic φροῦδος, *out of sight :* γῆν πρὸ γῆς ἐλαύνομαι, *I am driven onwards from one land to another.*

f. **Cause** or **Motive,** Latin *præ*—πρὸ φόβοιο, *through fear.*

SIGNIFICATIONS IN COMPOSITION.

a. **Advance,** in regard both to *place* and *time,* as in προτείχισμα, *an outwork :* προειπεῖν, *to speak before,* &c.

b. **Publicity**—as προϊέναι, *to come forward publicly.*

c. **Defence**—as in πρόμαχος.

d. **Preference**—as in προαιρεῖσθαι.

Under the head of Prepositions governing only a Genitive Case, may be classed ἕνεκα, with the meaning—*on account of, for the sake of, with respect to.*

§ 2. Prepositions governing only a Dative Case.

I. ἐν.

ἐν has the general meaning of IN, of a being or remaining WITHIN the compass of anything, and is used generally with Verbs of rest.

DERIVATIVE SIGNIFICATIONS.

a. **In,** of **place**—as ἐν ἀγορᾷ *in the Forum :* ἐν Σπάρτῃ *in Sparta.*

b. **In,** of **time**—as ἐν τούτῳ τῷ χρόνῳ, *within this time.*

c. **Amongst, in the number of**—as ἐν λῃσταῖς εἶναι, *to be among robbers.*

d. **In one's power**—Lat. *penes :* as ἐν σοι πᾶν τὸ πρᾶγμα, *everything depends on you.*

e. **In presence of** (really *amongst* as in (*c*))—λέγειν ἐν τῷ δήμῳ, *to speak in presence of the people.*

f. It is used with Nouns signifying *dress, arms,* &c.—as ἐν τῇ Περσικῇ στολῇ, *clad in a Persian robe :* ἐν ὅπλοις, *under arms.*

g. When used with Verbs signifying *motion,* it may be regarded as a *constructio prægnans.* Thus, ἐν χερσὶ λαβεῖν, *to take* (and hold) *in one's hand.*

h. The **means** or **instrument**—as σημαίνειν ἔν τινι, *to shew by something :* ὁρᾶν ἐν ὀφθαλμοῖς, *to see with the eyes.*

SIGNIFICATIONS IN COMPOSITION.

a. **Suitableness, correspondence** — as in ἔνδικος, ἔμμετρος, &c.

b. **Abatement** or **modification** of the word with which it is compounded—as ἔμπικρος, *somewhat bitter :* ἔνλευκος, *whitish :* ἐνδιδόναι, *to remit.*

PHRASES.

ἐν τάχει, *quickly.* ἐν καιρῷ, *opportunely.* ἐν ἑαυτῷ εἶναι, *to be in one's senses.* ἐν ὀργῇ ἔχειν τινα, *to make one an object of anger.* ἐν χρῷ κείρεσθαι, *to be shaven close to the skin.* οἱ ἐν γένει, *relations.*

II. σὺν or ξύν.

The general meaning of σὺν is WITH, in the sense of *community, conjunction.*

DERIVATIVE SIGNIFICATIONS.

a. **With the help of**—as σὺν 'Αθήνη, *with Minerva's help.*

b. **Agreement with**—as σὺν νόμῳ, *in accordance with law.*

c. **Manner**—as σὺν τάχει, σὺν βίᾳ ποιεῖν, *quickly, violently :* σὺν χρόνῳ, *at length.*

d. σὺν is frequently omitted, as in πλεύσαντες πέντε καὶ εἴκοσι ναυσί, *having sailed with five and twenty ships.*

SIGNIFICATIONS IN COMPOSITION.

Besides the general ideas of *communion, participation, conjunction,* &c. σὺν **intends** or **augments**—as in συντετα-μένως, *with concentrated force.*

§ 3. Prepositions governing only an Accusative Case.

I. ἀνά.

The general meaning of ἀνά is ON, UP (opposed to κατά with the accus.) It is used with a local Dative in Homer, Pindar, &c. as ἀνὰ σκήπτρῳ, *on a staff.*

DERIVATIVE SIGNIFICATIONS.

a. **Direction upwards**—ἀνὰ τὸν ποταμὸν πλεῖν, *to sail up the river.*

b. **Extension**—from bottom to top, and so **throughout**, with Verbs of rest as well as motion : ἀνὰ τὴν Ἑλλάδα, *throughout Greece.* So ἀνὰ δῆμον, *through all the people :* ἀνὰ τοὺς πρώτους εἶναι, *to be among the first :* ἀνὰ στόμα ἔχειν, *to have continually in the mouth.*

c. **Extension in time, duration**—ἀνὰ πᾶσαν τὴν νύκτα, *all the night through :* or, without the article, ἀνὰ πᾶσαν ἡμέραν, *every day :* ἀνὰ πᾶν ἔτος, *every year :* ἀνὰ χρόνον, *in course of time.*

d. With numbers, **up to**—ἀνὰ εἴκοσι μέτρα, *full twenty measures.*

e. **Distribution**—ἀνὰ πέντε παρασάγγας τῆς ἡμέρας, *five parasangs a-day.*

SIGNIFICATIONS IN COMPOSITION.

a. **Elevation**—as ἀναβαίνειν : ἀνέχειν τὰς χεῖρας, *to lift the hands.*

b. **Repetition**—as ἀναγράφειν, ἀναπλεῖν.

c. **Putting off, delaying**—as in ἀναβάλλειν.

d. As **Re**, in Latin—ἀναβλέπειν, *to recover one's sight.*

e. It **intends** or **augments**—as in ἀναπείθειν, ἀναβοᾶν.

PHRASES.

ἀνὰ κράτος, *vigorously.* ἀνὰ μέρος, *in turn.* ἀνὰ λόγον, *by argument,* or *in proportion.*

II. εἰς or ἐς.

This Preposition corresponds in its general meaning with the Latin *in* (with accus.) and signifies therefore INTO or UP TO, as εἰς τὴν πόλιν, *into the city.*

DERIVATIVE SIGNIFICATIONS.

a. It is used in a *hostile* sense—as ἐστράτευσαν εἰς τὴν Ἀττικήν, *they marched into,* or *invaded, Attica.*

b. **Extension through space**—as ἐκ θαλάσσης εἰς θάλασσαν, *from sea to sea.*

c. Lat. *coram*, with the idea of *direction towards* the object : and thus of *speaking to*, or *in presence of*—λόγους ποιεῖσθαι εἰς τον δῆμον, *to speak before the people.*

d. When used of time, it signifies either a *point* of time, **until**—as ἐς ἥλιον καταδύντα, *until sun set* : or *duration* of time—as ἐς θέρος, *for the summer :* εἰς ἐνιαυτόν, *for a year.*

e. **Intention, object**—as εἰπεῖν εἰς ἀγαθόν, *to speak for good :* εἰς τί; *for what ?* εἰς κέρδος τι δρᾶν, *to do anything for gain.*

f. Lat. *quod attinet ad,* **in respect to**—as διαφέρειν τινὸς εἰς ἀρετήν, *to excel one in virtue :* εἰς πάντα, *in every respect.*

g. In a *distributive* sense with numerals—as εἰς ἑκατὸν, *centeni :* εἰς δύο, *two and two :* also with numerals, **about, up to**—as ναῦς εἰς τὰς τετρακοσίας, *about four hundred ships.*

h. It is used elliptically with a Genitive—as εἰς ᾅδου sc. οἶκον, *to the abode of Pluto.*

SIGNIFICATIONS IN COMPOSITION.

a. **Motion into, direction towards**—as in εἰσάγειν, εἰσιέναι.

b. Bringing forward *in public*—as in εἰσφέρειν γνώμην.

c. **Acquisition**—as in εἰσποιεῖσθαι.

PHRASES.

ἐς καλόν, *opportunely.* εἰς τάχος, *quickly.* ἐς τὸ παραχρῆμα, *immediately.*

ὡς is used for εἰς, but only when motion towards *persons* is meant—as ἔπεμπον πρέσβεις ὡς τοὺς Ἀθηναίους, *they sent ambassadors to the Athenians.*

II. *Second Class.*

Prepositions governing two Cases.

The second Class contains four Prepositions, which govern a Genitive and an Accusative Case—*viz.* διά, κατά, μετά, ὑπέρ.

§ 1. διά.

The general meaning of διά is RIGHT THROUGH.

DERIVATIVE SIGNIFICATIONS.

I. With a Genitive.

a. **Through and out of**—as διὰ ὤμου ἦλθεν ἔγχος, *the spear passed through the shoulder and out at the other side.*

b. **Extension through space**—as διὰ πεδίου, *through the plain :* διὰ πολεμίας πορεύεσθαι, *to march through a hostile country.*

c. **Extension through time**—διὰ παντὸς τοῦ χρόνου, *throughout the whole time :* δι' ἡμέρης, διὰ βίου.

d. **Intervals of time**—as διὰ τρίτου ἔτους, *every third year :* and of **space**, as διὰ δέκα ἐπαλξέων, *every tenth battlement :* διὰ δέκα ἡμερέων ὁδοῦ, *at the distance of ten days' journey.*

e. It denotes the **means** or **cause**, according to the original force of *coming through and out of.* 1. The **agent** or **instrument**—as διὰ χειρῶν (for χερσὶ): δι' ἀγγέλου λέγειν, &c. 2. The **manner** and **way**—as διὰ σπουδῆς, *with earnestness, earnestly :* and so δι'οἴκτου λαβεῖν, *to pity* (Eur.): δι' ὀργῆς ἔχειν, *to be angry with* (Thuc.) 3. The **material** of which a thing is made, as δι' ἐλέφαντος, *of ivory.*

f. It conveys the notion of **pre-eminence**—(as in composition, διαφέρειν.) ὁ δ' ἔπρεπε καὶ διὰ πάντων, *he was distinguished throughout among all.*

II. With an Accusative.

a. **Extension throughout and over a space**—as διὰ κῦμ' ἅλιον, *over the sea-wave.*

b. **Extension through time**—as διὰ νύκτα.

c. **By means of**—νικῆσαι δι' 'Αθήνην, *to conquer by the aid of Minerva.*

d. Lat. *propter*—διὰ τοῦτο, *because of this.*

SIGNIFICATIONS IN COMPOSITION.

a. **Passage through** (of space)—as in διαβαίνειν : (of time) as διαβιοῦν : (of an action) as διαπράττειν, where it has the force of *completion.*

b. **Separation** (the Lat. *dis.*)—as διαγιγνώσκω, διατέμνω.

c. It **intends** or **augments**—as διϊσχυρίζεσθαι, *to affirm constantly :* διακυκᾶν, *to throw into utter confusion.*

d. **Eminence** or **excellence**—as in διαφέρειν.

PHRASES.

διὰ πόθου ἐλθεῖν (for ποθεῖν), *to regret.* διὰ τάχους, *quickly.* διὰ κενῆς, *rashly.* διὰ μέσου, *meanwhile.* διὰ τέλους, *perpetually.*

§ 2. κατά.

The general meaning of κατά is DOWN, DOWNWARDS, FROM ABOVE (Lat. *desuper.*)—as in βῆ δὲ κατ' οὐλύμποιο καρήνων, *he went down the summits of Olympus.*

DERIVATIVE SIGNIFICATIONS.

I. With a Genitive.

a. **Down into and under**—as κατὰ τῆς θαλάσσης, κατὰ γῆς.

b. **Concerning**—as ταῦτα κατὰ Περσῶν ἔχομεν λέγειν, *we have this much to say concerning the Persians.* It is however commonly used thus in a *hostile* sense : as κατά τινος εἰπεῖν, *to speak against any one.* (Cf. κατηγορεῖν, *to accuse*).

c. It is used in **impreoations** or **vows**—as *εὔχεσθαι κατά τινος,* the hands being laid *down upon* the victim.

II. With an Accusative.

a. As opposed to *ἀνά,* it signifies **motion downwards** —*κατὰ ῥόον, down the stream :* ἀνὰ *ῥόον, up the stream.*

b. **Extension through and over space**—as *καθ' Ἑλλάδα, κατὰ πᾶσαν τὴν γῆν.*

c. Hence it may be construed by the Prepositions **on, in, among, at, about, over,** &c.—*κατὰ πόντον, καθ' ὅμιλον, κατὰ στρατὸν, κατὰ θυμὸν, κατὰ φρένα,* &c.

d. **Opposite to**—as *κατὰ Μαλέαν.*

e. **Distributively**—as *κατὰ φῦλα, by tribes :* κατ' *ἄνδρα, man by man :* κατ' *ἐνιαυτὸν, year by year.*

f. **A purpose**—as *πλεῖν κατὰ πρῆξιν, to sail on business.*

g. Of *fitness,* **according to, agreeably to** —*κατὰ νόμον :* οὐ κατ' *ἄνθρωπον φρονῶν, not thinking as a man ought to think.* Especially thus after *ἢ than :* as *μεῖζον ἢ* κατ' *ἄνθρωπον φρονεῖν, to have too high thoughts for a man.*

h. Lat. **ob, propter**—as *κατὰ τὸ ἔχθος τὸ Θεσσαλῶν, owing to their hatred of the Thessalians.*

k. With numbers, it is often used as Lat. *circiter,* **about,** to denote indefiniteness : as *κατὰ ἑξηκόσια ἔτεα, about six hundred years* (more or less).

l. Of periods of time, it is used to signify **throughout, during**—as *κατὰ Ἄμασιν, about the time of Amasis :* (less definite in this sense than *ἐπὶ* with Genitive): *κατὰ τὸν πόλεμον, throughout the war.*

L

SIGNIFICATIONS IN COMPOSITION.

a. **Against**—as in καταγιγνώσκειν τινὸς θάνατον, *to condemn one to death.*

b. **Descent**—as in καταβαίνειν.

c. **Return, restitution**—as in κατιέναι : κατάγειν, *to restore an exile to his country.*

d. **Consumption, wasting**—as κατακυβεύειν, *to lose in dicing, to gamble away.*

e. It **intends** or **augments**—as in καταπράττειν, *to perform thoroughly* : καθορᾶν, *to see clearly.*

PHRASES.

κατὰ νώτου, *in the rear.* κατὰ μοῖραν, *rightly.* κατὰ καιρὸν, *opportunely.* κατὰ μικρὸν, *by degrees.* κατὰ κράτος, *with all one's might.* κατὰ μέρος, *in turn.* καθ' ὅλου, *in general.* καθ' ἡσυχίην, *i.e.* ἡσύχως, *quietly.* κατ' ἀρχὰς, *in the beginning.*

§ 3. ὑπέρ.

The general meaning of ὑπὲρ is OVER—Lat. *super.*

DERIVATIVE SIGNIFICATIONS.

I. With a Genitive.

a. **Over,** of an object *at rest*—ὑπὲρ κεφαλῆς, *over one's head* : ὑπὲρ θαλάσσης, of towns, &c. situated *over* or *near the sea.*

b. **Over,** of an object *in motion*—(chiefly *Poet.*) κῦμα νηὸς ὑπὲρ τοίχων καταβήσεται (*Hom.*) *the water will come in over the sides of the ship.*

c. For the *Lat.* **de,** *concerning,* especially by Demosthenes : ἀπολογεῖσθαι ὑπὲρ τούτων, *to offer a defence about these things.*

d. In the sense of *standing over, defending* a person. Thus, μάχεσθαι ὑπὲρ τῆς πατρίδος.

e. **Substitution for**—*i.e.* of one thing placed *over* another and substituted for it : as μὴ θνῆσχ' ὑπὲρ τοῦδ' ἀνδρός, *do not die for this man.* (*Eur.*) Χριστὸς ὑπὲρ ἡμῶν ἀπέθανε. (N.T.) *Christ died for us.*

f. The **cause** of an action, where ὑπό with Gen. is more usual : as ὑπὲρ πένθους, *from sorrow.*

g. With Verbs of entreating, **for the sake of**—as ὑπὲρ τοκέων λίσσομαι, *I entreat you for the sake of your parents.*

II. With an Accusative.

a. Generally of motion **over** or **beyond**—as ῥίπτουσιν ὑπὲρ τὸν δόμον, *they throw over the house :* ὑπὲρ δύναμιν, *beyond our powers.*

b. Where we should say **contrary to** or **against**—as ὑπὲρ μόλον, *contrary to fate :* ὑπὲρ ὅρκια, *contrary to the oaths :* ὑπὲρ Θεὸν, *against God's will.*

c. Of numbers—as ὑπὲρ πεντήκοντα ἔτη *over,* or, *more than fifty years.*

d. **After**—as ὑπὲρ τά μηδικὰ, *after the Persian war.*

Significations in Composition.

a. **Beyond** (of place)—as in ὑπερβαίνειν.

b. **Beyond** (of time)—as in ὑπέργηρως, *exceeding old.*

c. **Excess**—as in ὑπερχαίρειν.

d. **Passing over, neglecting,** and so **contempt**—as in ὑπερορᾶν : so ὑπερβαίνειν τὸν νόμον, *to despise, transgress, the law.*

e. **Protection**—as in ὑπερμαχεῖν.

f. **Superiority**—as in ὑπερβάλλειν.

§ 4. μετά.

The general idea of μετὰ (connected with μέσος), is that of being IN THE MIDST of something.

DERIVATIVE SIGNIFICATIONS.

I. With a Genitive.

a. **Association with**—μετὰ νεκρῶν κείσομαι, *I shall lie among the dead :* μετὰ κινδύνων τὰς μελετὰς ποιεῖσθαι, *to go through one's* (military) *practice in the midst of dangers.*

b. Hence **by the help of**—μετὰ θεῶν, *with the help of the gods.*

c. **In accordance with**—μετὰ τῶν νόμων, *according to the laws.*

d. **Though, by means of**—μετ' ἀρετῆς πρωτεύειν, *to excel through virtue.*

II. With an Accusative.

a. With Verbs of motion, **among, into the midst of,** especially among a *number of persons*— as ἱκέσθαι μετὰ Τρωας καὶ 'Αχαιούς : more rarely of *things,* as μετὰ νῆας. This is chiefly a Homeric usage.

b. It expresses the idea of **following after**—either (1) in a *friendly* or (2) *hostile* manner, or (3) *in search of.* (1). βῆναι μετὰ Ν'στορα, *to go to see Nestor.* (2). ὥστ' ἀιγυπιὸς μετὰ χῆνας, *like a vulture in pursuit of geese.* (3). πλεῖν μετὰ χαλκόν, *to sail in quest of brass.*

c. **Succession, next to**—ποταμὸς μέγιστος μετὰ "Ιστρον, *the greatest river next to the Danube.*

77

d. **After** (of time)—as μετὰ ταῦτα, *after this* : μετὰ Σόλωνα οἰχόμενον, *after the departure of* Solon.

e. Lat. *secundum,* **according to**—μετὰ σὸν καὶ ἐμὸν κῆρ.

μετὰ is also used with a Dative by the Poets, in the sense of— (1). **Among**—as μετ' ἀθανάτοις, *among the immortals.* μετὰ τριτάτοισιν ἄνασσεν, *among* the third, though he did not *belong* to it. This would be μετὰ τρίτάτων. (2). **Between**—as μετὰ χερσὶ, ποσσὶ, γένυσσι. (3). **Addition to**—as μετὰ τοῖσιν ἐλέγμην, *I chose myself to be added to their party.*

SIGNIFICATIONS IN COMPOSITION.

a. **Change**—as in μεταγινώσκω, μεταβαίνω, μεταδίδωμι.

b. **Participation, communion**—as in μετέχω, μεταδίδωμι.

c. An **interval** of space, time, &c.—μεταίχμιον, *the space between two armies* : μεταδόρπιος, *during supper.*

d. **Pursuit**—μεταδιώκω, μέτειμι.

e. Lat. **Re**—μετατρέπω, μεταστρέφω.

III. *Third Class.*

Prepositions governing three Cases.

The third Class contains six Prepositions, which govern a Genitive, a Dative, and an Accusative Case : *viz.* ἀμφὶ, περὶ, ἐπὶ, παρὰ, πρὸς and ὑπό.

§ 1. ἀμφὶ (Poët. ἀμφίς.)

The general meaning of ἀμφὶ is **on both sides of,** and hence **around.** It is closely connected with περί. ἀμφὶ is mostly confined to the Ionic Dialect, while περὶ is used in all the Dialects.

DERIVATIVE SIGNIFICATIONS.

I. With a Genitive (rarely in Prose).

a. Like ἕνεκα, **about, for the sake of**—μάχεσθαι ἀμφί τινος, *to fight for a thing.*

b. **About, concerning** (like περὶ with gen.)—as ἀμφὶ φιλότητος ἀείδειν, *to sing of love.*

c. **About,** (of place)—ἀμφὶ τῆς πόλεως οἰκεῖν, *to dwell around the city.*

II. With a Dative.

a. The usage of ἀμφὶ with a Dat. scarcely differs from that with a Gen. Thus, we have τελαμὼν ἀμφὶ στήθεσσι, *a belt around his breast :* ἀμφὶ πυρί, *on the fire :* ἀμφὶ κλάδοις ἕζεσθαι, *to sit among, surrounded by, branches :* ἀμφὶ νέκυϊ μάχεσθαι, *to fight for a dead body :* φοβηθεὶς ἀμφὶ τῇ γυναικὶ, *fearing for the safety of his wife.*

b. Sometimes, especially by the Poetic writers, it is used to signify **at** or **near**—ἀμφὶ δίναις Εὐρίπου, *near the whirlpools of the Euripus.*

c. To these may be added the peculiar usage, Lat. **præ**— ἀμφὶ φόβῳ—θυμῷ, *through fear—anger.*

III. With an Accusative (most usual in Prose.)

a. **Around, about**—as ἀμφὶ ῥέεθρα, *about or near the streams :* ἀμφὶ τὴν πόλιν, *about the city.*

b. **About,** as a loose definition of time, or number— ἀμφὶ πλειάδων δύσιν, *about the setting of the Pleiades :* ἀμφὶ δείλην, *about dusk :* ἦν ἀμφὶ τὰ τριάκοντα ἔτη, *he was about thirty years of age.*

c. As *Lat.* de—ἀμφὶ 'Ἴλιον ἄεισον ᾠδάν, *sing a song about Ilium.*

d. **Employment, pains,** about a thing—εἶναι, ἔχειν ἀμφί τι : ἀμφ' ἵππους, ἅρματα ἔχειν, *to be occupied with horses, chariots.*

Significations in Composition.

a. **About, on both sides**—as ἀμφίστομος, *double edged :* ἀμφικύπελλον, *a double cup :* ἀμφιλέγειν, *to argue on both sides.*

b. **Encompassing, enclosing**—as in ἀμφιβάλλειν.

Phrases.

οἱ ἀμφὶ Πλάτωνα, *Plato and his followers.*   τὰ ἀμφὶ τὸν πόλεμον, *i.e.* τὰ πολεμικὰ, *warlike affairs.*

§ 2. περί.

περὶ differs in its general signification from ἀμφὶ, in that it signifies **round, all around,** in reference to the *whole circumference,* whereas ἀμφὶ refers only to **both sides.** (See under ἀμφί.)

Derivative Significations.

I. With a Genitive.

a. περὶ is only used in Poetry, and that but seldom, in a *local* sense, with the Genitive—as in περὶ σπείους γλαφυροῖο *around a hollow cave.*

b. In a *causal* sense it is very frequently joined to this Case, and has the meaning of—1. **Concerning**—as -μερμηρίζειν περὶ τινος, *to be anxious about a thing.* 2. **For**—as in θνήσκειν περὶ τινος, *to die for one.* 3. *Lat.* **præ**—μάχεσθαι περὶ ἔριδος, *to fight out of enmity*. 4. Especially with Verbs of *hearing, declaring, knowing*, &c. **about** or **concerning** —as οἶδα περὶ κείνου, *I know about him :* λέγειν περί τινος, &c. 5. Lat. *quod attinet ad :* ἀριθμοῦ πέρι, *as to number.*

c. It denotes **worth, estimation, superiority**—as in περὶ πάντων ἔμμεναι ἄλλων, *to be superior to all others.* Hence the phrases ποιεῖσθαι περὶ πολλοῦ, πλείονος, οὐδενός, &c. *to set a high—more—no,* &c. *value on* (a person or thing.)

II. With a Dative.

a. Like ἀμφὶ, it denotes **around, round about,** but with the additional notion of *close* connection. Thus, περὶ κρατὶ, στήθεσσι, &c. in the sense (e. g.) of armour or dress *fitting close to the head, breast,* &c.

b. Hence the idea of *flesh closing round* the weapon that wounds it—as in ἀσπαίρειν περὶ δουρί, *to palpitate with the lance sticking in his body :* περὶ ξίφει, &c.

c. Like ἀμφὶ, it is causal, of an object **for** or **about,** which one *struggles, fears, takes courage,* &c. (in Prose in this sense it always take a Genitive. (See I, (*b.*)) as περὶ πατρίδι μαρνάμενος, δεδιὼς περὶ τῷ χωρίῳ, θαρρεῖν περί τινι, &c.

III. With an Accusative.

a. **Action, motion, about** or **near** (a point)—especially in describing events as occurring *near* a place. Thus, ἡ περὶ Κνίδον ναυμαχία, *the sea-fight near Cnidus :* περὶ φρένας ἦλυθ' ἰωή, *round his mind came the call.*

b. Without the idea of action or motion—as in ἑστάμενοι περὶ τοῖχον, *standing about the wall :* περὶ Πιερίην διέτριβε, *he used to live in Pieria.* Hence οἱ περὶ Πλάτωνα, *Plato and his scholars :* (see ἀμφὶ, Phrases.)

c. The *object* about which one is concerned—as in ἡ φιλο-
σοφία περὶ ἀλήθειάν ἐστι, *philosophy is concerned about truth :*
περὶ δόρπα πονεῖσθαι, *to be busy about dinner.*

d. To denote number and time *indefinitely*—as περὶ μυρίους,
about 10,000 : περὶ τούτους τοὺς χρόνους, *about these times.*

e. The *object* to which an action refers—as τὰ περὶ τὸν
Κῦρον, *matters referring to Cyrus:* αἱ περὶ τὸ σῶμα ἡδοναί, *the
pleasures of the body.*

SIGNIFICATIONS IN COMPOSITION.

a. **Circuit, round about**—as in περιβλέπειν.

b. It **intends or augments** in a good sense—as in περι-
καλλής, περιουσία: and in a bad sense, as in περιβόητος, *in-
famous :* περίεργος, *officious.*

c. **Contempt, negligence**—as in περιόπτεσθαι, περι-
φρονεῖν.

d. **Mastery, conquest**—as in περιγίγνεσθαί τινος.

§ 3. ἐπί.

The general meaning of ἐπί is UPON, ON. It expresses
originally the position of one thing *on* another.

DERIVATIVE SIGNIFICATIONS.

I. With a Genitive.

a. Of **place** in various relations—1. UPON, ON. Thus
οἱ ἄνδρες ἐπὶ τῶν κεφαλέων τὰ ἄχθεα φορέουσι, *the men bear
burdens on their heads :* ἐπὶ δίφρου, *in a chariot :* ἐφ' ἵππου, *on
horseback :* ἐπὶ τῶν θυρέων, *at the doors :* οἰκέωμεν ἐφ' ἡμέων
αὐτῶν, *let us live to ourselves :* i.e. *depending on* ourselves
alone.   To these may be added the phrases τετάχθαι ἐφ'

M

ἑνός, *to be drawn up in single file : ἐπὶ τεττάρων, four deep.*
2. *In presence of,* (especially of witnesses to an oath) : ἐπωμόσαντο ἐπὶ τῶν στρατηγῶν, *they swore in presence of the generals.* 3. *Over, of persons in authority over a thing—* as ὁ ἐπὶ τῶν ὅπλων, *he who has charge of the arms :* οἱ ἐπὶ τῶν πραγμάτων, *those entrusted with the management of affairs.* 4. *In the instance* or *case of—*ἃ ἐπὶ τῶν ἄλλων ὁρᾶτε, *what you see in the case of others.* 5. *Motion towards a place :* as πλεῖν ἐπὶ Σάμου, *to sail towards Samos :* just as we speak of an army marching *upon* a place.

b. Of **time,** *in* or *during* which something takes place— ἐπ' εἰρήνης, *in time of peace :* ἐπὶ Κύρου βασιλεύοντος, *in the reign of Cyrus :* ἐπ' ἐμοῦ, *in my time.*

c. Of the **occasion, grounds** on which a thing happens —ἐφ' ἑαυτοῦ, *of one's own accord :* εἰπεῖν ἐφ' ὅρκου, *to speak on oath :* so ἐπὶ Λυδοῦ τοῦ Ἄτυος ἔσχον τὴν ἐπωνυμίην, *they were called after Lydus, the son of Atys :* ἐπ' ὅτευ, *on what ground, wherefore.*

II. With a Dative.

a. Of place, **on**—κείμενος ἐπὶ τῇ πυρᾷ, *lying on the funeral pile :* or **at, by, near**—οἰκέοντες ἐπὶ Στρυμόνι, *living on* or *by the Strymon :* ἐπὶ τῇσι θύρῃσι, *at the doors :* οἱ ἐπὶ ταῖς μηχαναῖς, *those stationed at the engines.*

b. **Against**—ἐπὶ Τρώεσσι μάχεσθαι, *to fight against the Trojans.*

c. **Next to, after**—ἀνέστη ἐπὶ αὐτῷ, *he rose up after him.* Hence the idea of one thing *added to* another—as ἐσθίουσιν ἐπὶ τῷ σίτῳ ὄψον, *they eat meat on* or *with bread :* ἐπὶ τούτοις, *in addition to these things :* φόνος ἐπὶ φόνῳ, *murder after murder.*

d. It is used to denote **dependence**—as γίγνεσθαι ἐπί τινι, *to be under one's power :* τὸ ἐπί σοι, *as far as depends on you.*

e. **Over, in authority over**—ἐπὶ τοῖς πράγμασιν εἶναι, *to be at the head of affairs.*

f. **Condition, object**—ἐπὶ τούτῳ, *on this condition, or for this purpose :* ἐφ' ᾧτε, *on condition that :* ἐπ' ἐλευθερίᾳ, *on condition of freedom :* ἐπὶ μισθῷ, *for pay :* ἐπὶ θήρᾳ ἐξιέναι, *to go out hunting.*

g. **Ground** or **occasion** of a mental affection—χαίρειν ἐπί τινι, *to rejoice at a thing :* γελᾶν ἐπί τινι, *to laugh at one.*

h. **Price, reward, with a view to**—Thus, δώρῳ ἐπὶ μεγάλῳ, *with a view to a great reward :* ἄδειν ἐπὶ μόσχῳ, *to sing for the prize of a calf.*

i. Of **time, in** or **at** which a thing happens—ἐπὶ νυκτί, *in the night :* and *after,* as ἐπ' ἐξεργασμένοις, *after it was all over.*

III. With an Accusative.

a. **Motion towards** and **arrival at** a place—as ἀναβαίνειν ἐφ' ἵππον, *to mount on horseback :* καταφεύγειν ἐπὶ λόφον, *to flee to a hill.*

b. **Extension in space** or **time**—ἐπ' ἐννέα κεῖτο πέλεθρα, *he lay stretched over nine acres :* πλεῖν ἐπὶ οἴνοπα πόντον, *over the sea :* ἐπὶ πολλὰς ἡμέρας, *for many days.*

c. **Against** (in a hostile sense)—στρατεύεσθαι ἐπὶ Λυδούς, *to march against the Lydians.*

d. With numbers, **up to, nearly**—ἐπὶ τριηκόσια, *about three hundred.*

e. **Object, intention**—ἐπὶ θήραν ἰέναι, *to go hunting.* Hence ἐπὶ τί; *wherefore ?*

f. **Mode, manner**—ἐπὶ στάθμην, *according to rule.*

g. Lat. *quod attinet ad*—τὸ ἐπ' ἐμέ, *as far as I am concerned.*

SIGNIFICATIONS IN COMPOSITION.

a. **Hostility**—as in ἐπιτειχίζειν.

b. **Succession**—ἐπίγονοι, *descendants.*

c. **Addition to**—ἐπιδιδόναι : ἐπίκτητοι φίλοι, *newly acquired friends.*

d. **Continuance** or **duration** of time—ἐφημέριος, *continuing for one day only.*

e. **Distribution**—ἐπιδέκατος, ἐπόγδοος.

f. **Superintendence**—ἐπίσκοπος.

g. It **intends** or **augments**—ἐπιορκεῖν, ἐπιποθεῖν.

PHRASES.

ὡς ἐπὶ τὸ πολύ, *for the most part.* ἐπ' ἀληθείας, *of a truth, truly.* ἐπίπαν, *altogether.* ἐπ' ἴσα, *equally.* ἐπὶ χρόνον, *for a while.* ἐπ' ἐλαφρῷ, *easily.*

§ 4. παρά.

The radical signification of παρά is that of *proximity*—BESIDE, BY THE SIDE OF—chiefly of *persons.* (See under ἐκ.)

DERIVATIVE SIGNIFICATIONS.

I. With a Genitive.

a. **From by the side of** (cf. French, *de chez moi*) as ἐλθεῖν παρά τινος : φάσγανον ἐρύσσασθαι παρὰ μηροῦ, *to draw his sword from* (beside) *his thigh:* ἀγγελίη ἥκει παρὰ βασιλῆος, *a message is come from the king.*

b. It denotes the person or thing, whence *knowledge* or *information* proceeds ; and, generally, παρά τινος implies *all that issues from any one,* as (e. g.) commands, promises, gifts, &c. Thus, παρ' Αἰγυπτίων μεμαθήκασι, *they learnt from the Ægyptians :* παρ' ἑωυτοῦ διδούς, *giving from his own resources :* ἡ παρά τινος εὔνοια, *the favour of any one.*

II. With a Dative.

a. **Beside, along side of,** only with Verbs implying *rest*—ἔστη παρὰ τῷ βασιλεῖ, *he stood by the king:* παρὰ ταῖς ναυσί, *near the ships.*

b. Hence used of a person's *judgment,* or *opinion :* παρ' ἔμοιγε, *at least in my opinion :* παρ' ἐμοὶ κριτῇ, *coram me, me judice :* τοὺς παρὰ σφίσιν αὐτοῖσι δοκέοντας ὀλβίους, *those who are, in their own opinion, happy.*

III. With an Accusative.

a. **To by the side of,** with Verbs of motion—ἀφικέσθαι παρὰ Κροῖσον, *to come to Crœsus* (and stand by him).

b. Motion **along by** a place—as παρὰ θῖνα, *along the shore.* Hence the notion of going **by,** and **past, beyond** a place —as in παρὰ τὴν Βαβυλῶνα παριέναι, *to go, pass by Babylon.*

c. This idea of *beyond* easily leads to that of **contrary to, against**—as in παρὰ δύναμιν, *beyond one's strength :* παρὰ δόξαν, *contrary to one's opinion :* παρὰ μοῖραν, *contrary to destiny.*

d. **Besides**—παρὰ ταῦτα, *besides these things.*

e. **In comparison,** with the idea of things being placed *side by side*—παρὰ τὰ ἄλλα ζῶα, *compared with all other animals :* (Cf. Lat. *præ.*) Hence παρ' οὐδὲν ἡγεῖσθαι, *to think nothing of.* Connected with this, is the notion of *difference, i.e.* the measure of excess or defect, whereby a purpose exceeds or falls short of its accomplishment. Thus, παρὰ πολύ ἀμείνων, *far better :* παρὰ πολύ περιγίγνεσθαι, *to conquer by a great deal :* παρὰ μικρὸν ἦλθεν ἀποθανεῖν, *he came within a little of dying :* (Lat. *parum abfuit quin—*) παρὰ τρεῖς ψήφους μέτεσχε τῆς πόλεως, *he was within three votes of obtaining a share in the government.*

f. Hence the idea of *superiority*—παρὰ τοὺς ἄλλους πονεῖν, *to labour more than the rest.*

g. **On account of** (compare the vulgar English *along of*)—οἱ δὲ εὐέλπιδές εἰσι παρὰ τὴν ἐμπειρίαν, *they are in good hope owing to their experience.*

h. When used of time, it signifies (1) *duration* of time—παρὰ τὸν πόλεμον, *in the course of the war:* παρ' ὅλον τὸν βίον, *one's life long.* (2.) A *point* of time—παρ' αὐτὸν τὸν κίνδυνον, *in the moment of danger.* (3.) *Alternation*—as παρ' ἡμέραν, *day by day:* παρὰ τρίτην ἡμέραν, *every third day:* παρὰ μῆνα, *every other month.*

SIGNIFICATIONS IN COMPOSITION.

a. **Assumption**—as in παραλαμβάνειν.

b. **Passing beyond, transgression**— παραβαίνειν : Hence *contrary to* : as in παραίσιος, *contrary to fate.*

c. **Carelessness, negligence**—παρορᾶν, *to overlook.*

d. **Proximity**—παρακολουθεῖν, παρακαθῆσθαι.

e. **Departure**—παραχωρεῖν ὁδοῦ.

f. **Similitude**—παραπλησίως, παρόμοιος.

§ 5. πρός.

The primary meaning of πρός (which is derived from πρό) is BEFORE, IN FRONT OF, whence the three Cases signify generally—*Gen.* FROM (before a place) : *Dat.* NEAR, BY (a place): *Accus.* direction or motion TO or IN FRONT OF (a place).

DERIVATIVE SIGNIFICATIONS.

I. With a Genitive.

a. It denotes the *situation* of a place—as in πρὸς Νότου, *towards the south* (cf. *ab oriente*): *i.e.* **from**, in regard to motion commencing from the direction indicated, and **to-wards,** *going from,* in reference to ourselves. The same idea is of course expressed by the Accusative. In a passage in Herodotus (II. 121) both cases are given in the same sentence—τὸν μὲν πρὸς βορέω ἑστεῶτα, τὸν δὲ πρὸς νότον, *one standing towards the north, the other towards the south.*

b. **From, on the side of,** in reference to *relationship*— οἱ πρὸς αἵματος, *blood-relations :* οἱ πρὸς μητρὸς, *relations by the mother's side.*

c. It denotes **origin, authorship,** *and effects proceeding from any cause*—ἔχει τιμὴν πρὸς Διός *he has honour from,* or *at Jupiter's hands.* So παθεῖν τι πρός τινος, *to receive an injury from any one :* πρὸς Διός also signifies *by the will of Jupiter,* and *under Jupiter's protection.*

d. Hence the idea of **suitableness, conformity with** —πρὸς ἀνδρός ἐστι, *it belongs to a man, it is his duty :* ἄτοπα λέγεις, ὦ Σώκρατες, καὶ οὐδαμῶς πρός σου, (Plat.) *you speak absurdly, Socrates, and unworthily of yourself:* πρὸς δίκης ἐστί, *it is in accordance with justice.*

e. **On the side of,** *i.e. for one's advantage*—as πρὸς τῶν ἐχόντων, Φοῖβε, τὸν νόμον τίθης, *you enact a law, Phœbus, in favour of the rich :* εἶναι πρός τινος, *to be on one's side.*

f. **In the eyes of, before**—ἄδικον πρὸς Θεῶν, *unjust before the gods, i.e. in their presence.* So ἐπιορκεῖν πρὸς δαίμονος, *to forswear one's self by a god.*

g. Hence it is often used in *oaths* and *adjurations,* and signifies **by**—πρὸς θεῶν, *by the gods:* πρός τ' ἀλόχου καὶ πατρός, *by your wife and father :* usually with the Pronoun interposed, as πρός σε δεξιᾶς ἱκνοῦμαι, *I pray you by your right hand.*

II. With a Dative.

a. It expresses *rest* in front of, near or by an object—as πρὸς Βαβυλῶνι ἦν ὁ Κῦρος, *Cyrus was before Babylon :* πρὸς τοῖς κριταῖς, *before the judges.*

b. So of occupations—as πρὸς πράγμασι γίγνεσθαι, *to be engaged in business :* Cf. Eng. *at*, in the expression, *at work.*

c. In addition to—as πρὸς τούτοις, *besides this.*

III. With an Accusative.

a. To, towards (either with persons or things)—as in ἀπελθεῖν πρὸς τὸν Κῦρον, *to go to Cyrus :* προτὶ ἄστυ δύω κήρυκας ἔπεμπε, *he sent two heralds to the city.* So of *points of the compass*—as πρὸς ἔω, *eastward :* πρὸς βορέαν, *northward.*

b. Against, in a hostile sense—μάχη Περσῶν πρὸς 'Αθηναίους, *the fight of the Persians with the Athenians :* it is also used without this hostile signification, as in λέγειν πρός τινα, *to speak to, or towards, a person :* οὐδὲν πρός ἐμε, *it is nothing to me :* ἄδειν πρὸς αὐλὸν, *to sing to the flute.*

c. Relatively to—οὐδενὸς ἄξιος πρὸς σοφίαν, *worthless as regards wisdom :* and so of comparisons, as φαῦλοι πρὸς ἡμᾶς, *mean, compared with us.* In Herodotus, it is used of *superiority to,* as Ἰνδοὶ φόρον ἀπαγίνεον πρὸς πάντας τοὺς ἄλλους, *the Indians paid more tribute than all the rest :* and so of exchanges, as in ἡδονὰς πρὸς ἡδονὰς καὶ λύπας πρὸς λύπας, *pleasures against pleasures and sorrows against sorrows.*

d. It denotes a purpose—as in πρὸς φυλακὴν καὶ σωτηρίαν, *with a view to their defence and preservation.*

c. According to, agreeably with—πρὸς τοῦτο τὸ κήρυγμα, *according to this proclamation.* So κρίνειν τι πρός τι : πρὸς ταῦτα, *accordingly.*

f. It denotes an indefinite point of *time*—as in πρὸς ἡμέραν, *towards daybreak.* So of *number* : as πρὸς ἑκατόν, *towards a hundred.*

SIGNIFICATIONS IN COMPOSITION.

a. **Motion towards**—as in προσέρχεσθαι.

b. **Addition to**—as in προσερωτᾶν, *to ask besides.*

c. **Proximity**—as in προσκαθίζεσθαι, *to sit down near.*

d. It **intends** or **augments**—as in προσαιτεῖν, *to beg hard.*

PHRASES.

πρὸς βίαν, *violently.* πρὸς φιλίαν, *in a friendly manner.* πρὸς καιρὸν or ὥραν, *seasonably.* πρὸς ὕβριν, *insolently.* πρὸς ὑπερβολὴν, *surpassingly, exceedingly.*

§ 6. ὑπό.

The primary meaning of ὑπὸ is UNDER.

DÉRIVATIVE SIGNIFICATIONS.

I. With a Genitive.

a. Motion from under—**from below, out from under**—ἡ πηγὴ ὑπὸ τῆς πλατάνου ῥεῖ, *the fountain flows from under the plane-tree.*

b. Simply of *rest under,* where the Dat. is more usual—as in ὑπὸ γῆς οἰκεῖν, *to dwell under the earth.*

c. It denotes **the agent,** especially with Passive Verbs—as in κτείνεσθαι ὑπό τινος, *to be killed by some one.*

d. **The cause, actuating influence**—as in ὑπὸ τῆς παρεούσης συμφορῆς *under the influence of the present misfortune.* So ὑπ' ὀργῆς, *through anger :* ὑπὸ δέους, *through fear :* ὑπὸ κέρδους, *under the influence of gain.*

N

e. An *intermediate* cause, means or instrument—as in ὤρυσσον ὑπὸ μαστίγων, *they dug under the lash*: especially thus of the cheering, quickening influence of music—as in ἐστρατεύοντο ὑπὸ συρίγγων, *they marched to the sound of pipes.*

f. It expresses **subjection**—as in ἀρετῶσιν ὑπ' αὐτοῦ, *they are virtuous under his sway.*

II. With a Dative.

a. **Under,** without motion—as in ὑπὸ γῇ εἶναι, *to be under the earth*: ὑπὸ Τμώλῳ, *at the foot of Mount Tmolus.*

b. It is used in a *causal* sense, like the Gen.—as in δαμῆναι ὑπό τινι: ἐμῆς ὑπὸ χερσὶ δάμασσον, *subdue him under,* or *by, my hands.* So (as in Gen.)—ὑπὸ βαρβίτῳ, ὑπ' αὐλῷ χορεύειν, *to dance to the sound of the lyre* or *flute.*

e. **Subordination**—as in ὑφ' ἑαυτῷ εἶναι, *to be under one's own controul.*

III. With an Accusative.

a. **Motion to and under**—as in ὑπ' Ἴλιον ἦλθον, *they went to Troy* (*i.e.* under its walls). So ἰέναι ὑπὸ γῆν: ὑπὸ τοὺς Ἐφόρους (ἄγειν τινά) *to bring one before* (*i.e.* under the judgment seat of) *the Ephori.*

b. **Extension under an object**—ὑπέστιν οἰκήματα ὑπὸ γῆς, *there are habitations under the earth.*

c. It denotes time approximately—as in ὑπὸ νύκτα (Lat. *sub noctem*) *towards night*: it is used also of *extension* of time: as ὑπὸ τὴν νύκτα, *during the night.*

d. **Subordination**—as in ὑπὸ χεῖρα ποιεῖν, *to bring into subjection.*

SIGNIFICATIONS IN COMPOSITION.

a. **Under, beneath**—as in ὑπόγειος, *under the earth.*

b. **Secretly, by stealth**—as in ὑπεξαιρεῖσθαι, *to take away by stealth.*

c. It has a *diminuent* force—as in ὑπέρυθρος, *somewhat red* : ὑπόλευκος, *whitish.*

d. **Subjection**—as γυνὴ ὕπανδρος, *a wife in subjection to her husband.*

Certain Adverbs and some oblique Cases of Nouns used adverbially, are employed as Prepositions. The following govern a Genitive Case. 1. πρόσθεν, ἔμπροσθεν, *before.* 2. ὅπισθεν, *behind.* 3. εὐθὺ, *straight to.* 4. ἐνάπιον, *in presence of.* 5. ἄνευ, χωρὶς, *without.* 6. πλὴν, *except.* 7. μέταξυ, *between.* 8. μεχρὶ, *until.* 9. χάριν, *for the sake of.* Also with the possessive Pronouns—as in ἐμὴν, σὴν χάριν, *for my, your sake.* 10. δίκην, *in the way of, after the manner of.* 11. ἄντα, ἄντια, ἀντικρὺ, ἐνάντιον, used in the local sense of ἀντί. Only one governs a Dative— ἅμα, *with, at the same time with.*

PART V.

ON THE GREEK ACCENTS.

§ 1. GENERAL REMARKS.

1. PORSON recommends a careful study of the Greek Accents, in the following passage from a note on the first line of the *Medea*.

" Vos autem, adolescentes, vos nunc alloquor. Si quis
" vestrûm ad accuratam Græcarum literarum scientiam
" aspirat, is probabilem sibi accentuum notitiam quàm ma-
" turrimè comparet, in propositoque perstet, scurrarum
" dicacitate et stultorum irrisione immotus; ' *Nam risu*
" *inepto res ineptior nulla est.*' "

2. To this nothing need be added by way of recommenda-
tion to the acquirement of a thorough knowledge of Greek
Accentuation. That it is impossible to become an accurate
Greek Scholar without it, is evident from the fact that are
in Greek many words and forms of different significations,
which, being otherwise written alike, are distinguished *only*
by their accents.

93

3.. Accents were not used in ancient Greece, but are said to have been invented by Aristophanes of Byzantium, who, about the year B.C. 200, in the reigns of Ptolemy II. and Ptolemy III., lived in Alexandria as superintendent of the library.* They were probably intended for the use of strangers learning Greek, to assist them, in some way unknown to us, in the pronunciation.

4. It has been satisfactorily proved that they had nothing to do either with music or quantity. They served only to mark the *stretch* or pitch ($\tau\acute{o}\nu o\varsigma$) of the voice, at which the syllables were pronounced.

§ 2. Definitions and General Rules.

5. There are three accents—the **acute** ($\acute{o}\xi\upsilon\varsigma$ $\tau\acute{o}\nu o\varsigma$) marked ($\acute{a}$): the **grave** ($\beta\alpha\rho\grave{\upsilon}\varsigma$ $\tau\acute{o}\nu o\varsigma$) marked ($\grave{a}$): and the **circumflex** ($\pi\epsilon\rho\iota\sigma\pi\acute{\omega}\mu\epsilon\nu o\varsigma$) marked ($\tilde{a}$).

6. The acute is often called *the accent*, by way of eminence.

7. Accents are placed, of course, only on vowels and diphthongs. When a diphthong is accented, the accent stands on the second vowel, as $\mu o\acute{\upsilon}\sigma\alpha\iota\varsigma$, $\mu o\tilde{\upsilon}\sigma\alpha\nu$. When it falls on the first syllable of a word beginning with a vowel, it is placed, if an acute, immediately *after* the breathing : if a circumflex, *above* it : as $\check{\epsilon}\chi\omega$, $\epsilon\tilde{\iota}\chi o\nu$.

8. The grave is never expressed in writing, except on the last syllable of a word in the.middle of a sentence. Even there it is to be regarded as a *modified acute ;* for when such

---

* Smith's Dict. of Greek and Roman Biography, vol. 1, p. 215. Goettling, p. 10.

a word occurs before a full stop, or a colon, or note of interrogation, or even (according to Reiz) before a comma, the
acute is substituted for the grave. Thus, ὁ Θεὸς ἀγαθός
ἐστι : but ἀγαθός ἐστιν ὁ Θεός, where observe the different
accentuation of Θεός in the *middle*, and at the *end* of a
sentence.

9. The grave accent is *understood* on all syllables which
have neither the acute nor the circumflex. Thus, we write
ανθρωπος, not ἄνθρὼπὸς. The grave may indeed be regarded
merely as a *negation* of the acute.

10. The circumflex is formed from the union of the acute
and grave accents.* Thus, μουσέων, μουσῶν : φιλέοντα,
φιλοῦντα.

11. Whereas the acute may stand on any syllable, long or
short, the circumflex can only stand on a syllable *long by
nature*. A syllable long only by position is not circumflexed.
Thus, πρᾶγμα, because here (α) is long by nature : but
τάγμα, because (α) in this word, though long by position, is
short by nature.

12. All words have a single accent—*i.e.* either an acute or
a circumflex, of their own. This is strictly true, and without exception, of words *taken separately* : but, in continued
discourse, and under certain conditions, the words termed
Atonics (or *Proclitics*), and *Enclitics* (see § 11 and § 12) have
no accent, and words preceding Enclitics receive two accents.

---

* Not, observe, from the union of the *grave* and *acute*. Thus, θήρα arises
from the contraction of θέέρα, where the grave disappears, and the acute
only remains. Similarly ἐσταὼς is contracted into ἐστώς, not into
ἐστῶς.

13. A word having the acute on the last syllable is said to be **Oxytone,** as *ἰχθρός*.

14. A word having the acute on the penultima is said to be **Paroxytone,** as λόγος.

15. A word having the acute on the antepenultima is said to be **Proparoxytone,** as ἔτυπτε.

16. A word having the circumflex on the last syllable is ● said to be **Perispomenon,** as φιλῶ.

17. A word having the circumflex on the penultima is said to be **Properispomenon,** as σῶμα.*

18. Words that are not acuted or circumflexed on the last syllable are called **Barytones,** the grave being (by Rule 9) *understood* on that syllable.

19. **N.B.—If the last syllable be long, the word cannot be either Proparox. or Properisp. If the last syllable be short, it may bear either of these accents.**

20. **N.B.—No word can bear the acute beyond the antepenultima, or the omfix. beyond the penultima.†**

21. The terminations αι, οι, are considered *short* in accentuation. Thus, μοῦσαι, τύψασαι, ἄνθρωποι. Except in the

---

* As these words will frequently occur in the following Rules, they will be expressed hereafter by contractions: *viz. Oxyt.* for Oxytone, *Parox.* for Paroxytone, *Proparox.* for Proparoxytone, *Perisp.* for Perispomenon, *Properisp.* for Properispomenon, *Cmfx.* for Circumflex.

† In the following Rules, when the accent stands *as far back* as Rules 19 and 20 admit of its doing, the accentuation of the word will be said to be *regular.*

third pers. sing. of the Optat. Act. where *αι*, *οι*, have arisen from the old forms *παιδεύσαι*(*τ*)*ι*, *παιδεύσοι*(*τ*)*ι*, by contraction.

N.B.—*φίλησαι*, is 1 *Aor. Midd. Imper.* *φιλῆσαι*, 1 *Aor. Act. Infin.* *φιλήσαι*, 1 *Aor. Opt.* 3d *Sing.* (See Rule 44.)

22. The terminations *ως*, *ων*, in the fourth (Attic) declension of Simples, and in the second of Contracts, are also considered short. Thus, *Μενέλεως*, *ἀνώγεων*, *πόλεως*, *πήχεων*. The reason is, that the two Vowels '(*εω*) are regarded, and were, no doubt, formerly *pronounced*, as one. The same rule holds of compounds of *γέλως*, *κέρας* and *ἔρως*, as *φιλόγελως*, *εὔκερως*, *δύσερως* (pronounced probably *φιλόγ'λως*, &c.)

23. In *contractions—a.* If neither of the uncontracted Vowels is accented, the accent remains on the same syllable as before. Thus, *φίλεε*, *φίλει* (but *φιλέει*, *φιλεῖ*) : *ἀοιδή*, *ᾠδή*.

Except the **c**ontracted forms of some adjectives in *εος*, as *χρύσεος* *χρυσοῦς*, *χρύσεα χρυσᾶ (neut. plur.)* So also *κάνεον κανοῦν*.

b. If either of the Vowels to be contracted is accented, the accent generally remains on the contracted syllable. It will depend however on the preceding rules, which accent is to be used, circumflex or acute. Thus, *φιλέομεν*, *φιλοῦμεν*— *φιλεόμεθα φιλούμεθα*—*φιλεόντων φιλούντων* (Rule 19)—*τιμάω τιμῶ*, *βεβαὼς βεβώς*. (Rule 10 and Note.)

Except the nom. dual of contracts of the second declension, as *νόω νώ*, *ὀστέω ὀστώ*: the Gen. and Dat. Sing. of compounds in *οος*, as *ἀγχίνου*, *ἀγχίνῳ* from *ἀγχίνοος*—*ους*: the Gen. Plur. of adjectives in *ηθης*, of *τριήρης* and *αὐτάρκης*, as *συνήθων*, *τριήρων*, *αὐτάρκων*: the Gen. Sing. of the Attic declension, and the Accus. of the fourth of Contracts, as *λεάω λεώ*, *φειδόα*, *φειδώ*.

§ 2. Accentuation of Nouns Substantive.

24. As a general rule, in the oblique cases of nouns, the *same* accent remains on the *same* syllable as in the nominative, unless where one of the preceding rules would be violated by its so remaining. Thus, ἄνθρωπος, ἄνθρωποι, but ἀνθρώπων : σῶμα, σώματος, but σωμάτων : οἶκος, οἶκον, but οἴκου : ὁδοὺς, ὁδόντος : πρᾶγμα, πράγματος.

25. The gen. plur. of words of the first and second declensions is an exception, being always circumflexed. Since however it arises from contraction, the exception is only apparent. Thus, ταμιάων ταμιῶν : μουσάων μουσῶν.

Except the gen. plur. of ἀφύη, ἐτησίαι, χρήστης—*viz.* ἀφύων, ἐτησίων, χρήστων.

26. In the first four declensions the genitives and datives of all oxytone words are circumflexed.

Thus, 1. ποιητὴς, ποιητοῦ, ποιητῇ, ποιηταῖν, ποιητῶν, ποιηταῖς.
——— 2. ᾠδὴ, ᾠδῆς, ᾠδῇ, ᾠδαῖν, ᾠδῶν, ᾠδαῖς.
——— 3. καιρὸς, καιροῦ, καιρῷ, καιροῖν, καιρῶν, καιροῖς.
——— 4. λεὼς, λεῷ, (dat. sing.) λεῷν, λεῶν, λεῷς.

The genitive of the fourth declension is an exception, being oxyt.—as λεώ. All the other cases retain the accent of the nom. The cmflx. in every case arises from contraction : (e. g.) ᾠδῆς fr. ᾠδήος : καιροῦ fr. καιρόο : λεῷς fr. λεώις, &c.

27. In imparisyllabic monosyllables, the *genitives* and *datives* of all numbers are accented on the last syllable. The other cases follow Rule 24. Thus, μὴν, μηνὸς, μηνὶ, μηνοῖν, μηνῶν, μησί : but μῆνα, μῆνε, μῆνες, μῆνας.

Except the following—κῆρος (fr. κῆρ, *the heart*) : ἦρος (fr. ἦρ, *spring*) : υἶος (fr. υἶς, *a son*) : παίδων παίδοιν (fr. παῖς, *a son*) : θώων (fr. θώς, *a jackal*): κράτων (fr. κράς, *the head*) : σέων (fr. σής, *a moth*) : δᾴδων (fr. δαῖς δᾳς, *a torch*) : ὤτων (fr. οὖς *the ear*): φώτων (fr. φῶς, *light*.)

28. Imparisyllabic words of more than one syllable, if oxytoned, retain the accent throughout on the same syllable as in the nominative. Thus, φροντὶς φροντίδος, σφραγὶς σφραγῖδος, ἀγὼν ἀγῶνος, ποιμὴν ποιμένος.

29. Words of this declension that suffer *syncope* follow Rule 27. Thus, πατὴρ πατέρος πατρὸς, ἀνὴρ ἀνέρος ἀνδρός. θυγάτηρ and μήτηρ, though parox. in the nom., accent the oblique cases like πατήρ. Thus, θυγατρός, μητρός. The cases that are not syncopated take the accent on ε, wherever it appears. Thus, πατέρα, μητέρες, θυγατέρας. γυνὴ is irregularly accented. Thus, γυνὴ, γυναικὸς, γυναικὶ, γυναικοῖν, γυναικῶν, γυναιξί; but γυναῖκα, γυναῖκες, γυναῖκας. The vocatives of these words throw back their accent as far as possible. Thus, πάτερ, μῆτερ, θύγατερ.

30. The accentuation of the nominative singular of nouns must be learnt by careful observation. Goettling gives complete lists (pp. 111—278) of the accents of particular terminations of substantives, which are condensed in Jelf's Grammar, vol. 1, pp. 49—58. The following are a few of them, with such exceptions as are of frequent occurrence.

1. *Oxytone terminations.*—η ρ (exc. μήτηρ, θυγάτηρ), η ν, ε υ s, υ s, (gen. υος, exc. βότρυς, νέκυς, στάχυς), ι s (gen. ινος), ι s (gen. ιδος or ιτος, exc. ἔρις, θέμις, μῆνις), α s (gen. αδος), χ η (exc. μάχη, τύχη), ρ α (exc. ἕδρα, μοῖρα), μ η (exc. κόμη, τόλμη), δ η (exc. πέδη, ἀδελφιδῆ), γ η (exc. ἁρπάγη, στέγη, γῆ).

2. *Paroxytone terminations.*—ε α (exc. γενεά, δωρεά, θεά *a goddess*) : ι α (exc. λαλιά, σκιά, στρατιά and all feminines in τρια), ε ι α (exc. παρειά, χρειά, and derivatives from nouns in ε υ s or η s, whereof there is no verb in εύω), κ η (exc. ἀλκή, ἀκή, φυλακή), λ η (exc. nouns in ολή,

ωλή; and αὐλή, βουλή, κεφαλή, σχολή, φυλή), ν η (exc. nouns in ονή, and γύνη, εὐνή, σκηνή, φωνή), ξ α (exc. ἄμαξα), ο α (exc. στοά), π η (exc. σιωπή), τ η (exc. ἀρετή, ἑορτή, τελευτή). a s (gen. ου), η s (gen. ητος, exc. βραδυτής, ἐσθής), υ (exc. μῶλυ), ξ, (polysyllables, exc. αὔλαξ, κλῖμαξ, χοῖνιξ), ω ρ (gen. ρος, exc. ἰχώρ). Most of the other terminations are regular.

§ 3. Accentuation of Nouns Adjective, Numerals, and Pronouns.

31. Adjectives and pronouns, as a general rule, are accented as substantives; *i.e.* they retain the accent in the oblique cases on the same syllable as in the nom. sing. masc. The feminines of adjectives of three terminations, and of participles, are declinéd exactly like μοῦσα, and cmflx. the genitive plural. Thus, χαρίεις, χαρίεντος, χαριεσσῶν: τυφθείς, τυφθέντος, τυφθεισῶν.

32. *Barytone* adjectives and participles in ος do not circumflex the gen. plur. fem. Thus, ἅγιος, τυπτόμενος, gen. plur. fem. ἁγίων, τυπτο-μένων. Adjectives in ων, and parox. adjectives in ης (exc. those in ηρης, ωης, ωλης, ωρης and ωδης), throw back the accent in the neut. sing. and vocative. Thus, εὔδαιμον fr. εὐδαίμων: αὐτάρκης, αὔταρκες; but κωτήρης, κωπήρες. The neuter of *participles* in ων retains the accent on the same syllable as the masc., which, if long by nature, is circumflexed; if short, acuted. Thus, λαμβάνον, βουλεῦον, φιλέον (φιλοῦν.)

33. Comparatives and superlatives are regular.

34. εἷς *one*, in masc. and neut., follows the general rule for monosyllables (Rule 27.) The feminine is irregularly accented. Thus, μία, μιᾶς, μιᾷ, μίαν: δύο has gen. δυοῖν, δυσί: so ἄμφω, ἀμφοῖν: τρεῖς, τριῶν, τρισὶ, τρία: τέσσαρες, τεσσάρων, τέσσαρσι. The other cardinals, except ἑπτά, ὀκτώ, ἐννέα, ἑκατόν, are regular. N.B.—μύριοι means *ten thousand*: μυρίοι any indefinitely large number.

35. The ordinals, (from 1 to 19), are regular. All that end in οστος are oxyt. Thus, τέταρτος, but εἰκοστός.

36. Of ἐγὼ and σύ, the gen. sing., gen. dual, and all the cases of the plural are circumflexed. The other cases are oxyt.

37. The adjective pronouns are accented as follows—ἐμός, σός (Poët. τεός), αὐτός, ἐκεῖνος. All the rest are regular. τὶς indefinite is enclitic : τίς interrogative, retains the acute in all its cases.

38. *Oxytone terminations of adjectives.*—γ o s, (exc. ὀλίγος), κ o s, λ σ s (exc. ἄλλος, ὅλος, φίλος and forms of μέγας, as μεγάλοι), μ o s (with long penult. exc. ἔρημος, ἕτοιμος), ν o s (with long penult. exc. ἀγχιστῖνος, ἐκεῖνος) ω π o s, ρ o s, (exc. words in τερος, and ἄκρος, ἐλεύθερος, πόνηρος, μόχθηρος), σ o s (exc. μέσος, πόσος), τ o s (exc. the ordinals from 1 to 19, see Rule 35). υ s (gen. εος, exc. ἥμισυς, θῆλυς, πῆχυς.)

Paroxytone Terminations.—ε ι s (gen. εντος), ω s (gen. ωτος), ω ν (gen. οντος, exc. ἐκών). Compounds in ος used actively are parox. as παιδοκτόνος, *killing a son :* (παιδόκτονος would be—*killed by a son.*) Also in τ ε o s, as πρακτέος. Most other adjectives are regular.

§ 4. Accentuation of Verbs.

39. As a general rule verbs throw back their accent as far as possible.

40. Contractions of course modify the general rule ; but they can scarcely be regarded as exceptions, for when resolved, they present no anomaly. Thus, κρινῶ (1st fut. of κρίνω, contracted from κρινέσω κρινέω), φιλῶ (contracted from φιλέω), τιμᾶτον (contracted from τιμάετον). The same may be said of the subjunctives of passive aorists, as τυφθῶ, τυπῶ : of the optatives and subjunctives of verbs in μι, as τιθεῖμεν, τιθεῖτε, τιθεῖεν : τιθεῖο, τιθεῖτο, &c.

τιθῶ, *τιθῶμαι, &c. : of the 2 aor. imper. midd.† τυποῦ : and of many other instances in which the cmflx. has evidently arisen from contraction.

41. The Attic future is always circumflexed, as σκεδῶ, τελῶ, κομιῶ (§ 55, Gr. Gr.)

42. The 2 aor. inf. act. is always circumflexed, as τυπεῖν. The 2 aor. inf. midd. is parox. as τυπέσθαι.

43. The perf. pass. inf. is always parox. or properisp. τετύφθαι, πεποιησθαι.

44. The three forms mentioned in Rule 21, must be carefully noted, as they are distinguished solely by the accent. Thus, the 1 aor. inf. act. always accents the penult. with an acute, if *short*, with a cmflx., if *long* by nature, as φιλῆσαι ; but νομίσαι. The third pers. of all active optatives in αι and οι accents the penult. with the acute only, as φιλήσαι, φιλήσοι. The imper. 1 aor. midd. is regular, as φίλησαι.

N.B.—It is evident that some words must have the same accent for these three forms of the first aor. act. Thus, τύψαι for all three : since (υ) cannot be circumflexed in the 1 aor. infin. act., as being short by nature, though long by position.

45. All infinitives in ναι are parox. or properisp. as διδόναι, τετυφέναι, εἶναι, τυφθῆναι.

Except the old infinitives in ναι, as ἔμμεναι, δόμεναι, τυπήμεναι.

---

* Except δύνωμαι, ἐπίστωμαι, κρέμωμαί, &c. because (see Goettling, p. 80) derived from deponents, which have dropped their characteristic vowels, and so do not take the contracted form. The same remark applies to the optatives, δύναιτο, ἐπίσταιτο.

† Except *in composition*, when the accent is thrown back : as in προσγένου, ἐπιλάθου, ἀφίκου, ἐκβάλου : ἰδού, used as an interjection—*ecce !* is oxyt.

46. The 2 aor. imper. midd. of verbs in μι is circumflexed in the simple form, and also when compounded with *monosyllabic* prepositions—as θοῦ, δοῦ, ἐνθοῦ, προδοῦ. When comp. with *dissyllabic* prepositions, they are parox., as ἀπόδου, κατάθου.

47. The 2 aor. imperatives εἰπέ, ἐλθέ, εὑρέ, are oxyt. in all the dialects, and ἰδέ, λαβέ by the Attics. In composition, the accentuation of these words is regular, as ἀπόειπε, ἀπόλαβε.

48. In the pres. indic., verbs in μι are regular, as τίθημι. The only exceptions are the enclitics φημί and εἰμί (see § 12). These verbs make in the second pers. sing. φῄς, εἶ. In composition, they become regular, as σύμφημι, σύνειμι, σύμφῃς, σύνει, &c.

49. Compounds of the 2 aor. imperatives δός, σχές, θές, ἕς, are parox. as ἀπόδος, ἐπίσχες, κατάθες, μέθες.

50. The augment draws the accent as near to itself as possible: but in compound words the accent can never be thrown back *past* the augment. Thus, κατέσχον, παρῆλθον, παρῆν, ἐπέσπον, ἐπέβαν, ἀμφέσταν.

51. When the augment is dropped, the accent goes back to the preposition. Thus, σύνοιδα, κάτεχε (for κατεῖχε), ἔμβαλε (for ἐνέβαλε), κάββαλε (for κατέβαλε), πρόσβη (for προσέβη).

§ 5. Accentuation of Participles.

52. The 2 aor. act. both of verbs in ω and μι, all participles ending in εις, ως, and the present participles of verbs in μι, are oxyt., as τυπών, δούς, τυφθείς, τετυφώς, ἱστάς, δεικνύς.

53. Participles of perf. pass. are parox., as τετυμμένος, as likewise are 1 aor. act. participles (ας, for αις, being long) as φιλήσας.

54. ἰών (fr. εἶμι ibo) ·κιών, ἐών (for ὤν, fr. εἰμί sum), though not aorists, are oxyt., and the 2 aorists πέφνων, πίτνων, ὅφλων, θίγων, σχέθων, are exceptions to Rule 52.

55. ἀκαχήμενος, ἀλαλήμενος, ἀλιτήμενος, ἀρηρέμενος, ἐληλάμενος, ἥμενος, ἐσσύμενος, are exceptions to Rule 53.

56. In their *declension*, participles conform to the general rules for nouns (Rule 24, 28.) One exception—*viz.* that the fem. gen. plur. of participles in os is not circumflexed—is noticed in Rule 32. It must be observed also, that monosyllabic participles do not conform to Rule 27. Thus, δούς, δόντος, δόντι, δόντων, &c. *not* δοντός, δοντί, &c. the oblique cases being parox. instead of oxyt. and circumflexed. See also Rule 32, for the accentuation of the neuter of participles in ων.

§ 6. Accentuation of Adverbs.

57. Adverbs in ως, from adjectives in ος, follow the accent of the adjectives, ος oxyt. becoming ῶς circumflexed, and ος parox. or proparox. becoming ως parox. Thus, σοφός, σοφῶς: ἴσος, ἴσως: ὅρθιος, ὀρθίως.

58. Adverbs in ως from adjectives in υς are parox., as γλυκύς, γλυκέως.

59. Adverbs in θ α, δ α, ι, υ, δ ο ν, δ ι ς (if of more than three syllables and with long penult.) α ς, ξ, ψ, are *oxytone*. Adverbs in ι ν δ α, ω, δ η ν, ρ, α κ ι ς, ι κ α, δ ι ς (if of three syllables and with short penult.): genitive and dative-adverbs in θ ι, φ ι (φ ι ν,) θ ε (θ ε ν) if with short penult. are *paroxytone*. Genitive-adverbs in ο υ (as ὑψοῦ) and dative-adverbs in ο ι (as Πυθοῖ) are circumflexed. Most others are regular.

60. Accusative-adverbs in δε or ζε are accented according to the rule for enclitics. (See Rule 87, note.)

61. The monosyllabic particles μή, ναί, νή, δαί, μήν, δή, γάρ, μέν, δέ, ἄν, μά, πλήν, πρίν, are *oxytone*. πῆ, ποῖ, ποῦ, πῶς, μῶν, οὖν, αὖ, γοῦν, νῦν, are *circumflexed*. Observe the accents if ἵνα, δῆτα, οὕνεκα, μάλα, εἶτα, ὄφρα, ἔμπα, ἀλλά, ὅτι, ὅτε, τότε, ἔτι, εἴτε, ἕως, ὅπως, αὐτάρ.

62. Interjections ending in a long vowel or diphthong are circumflexed, as φεῦ, ὀτοτοῖ, ἰαῦ, παπαῖ. Those ending in consonants are oxyt. as βαβαιάξ, βομβάξ.

§ 7. Accentuation of Prepositions.

63. All the prepositions are oxyt. except ἐν, εἰς, ἐξ and ὡς for πρός, which are Atonic. (See Rule 82.)

64. Dissyllabic prepositions set after their case, throw back their accent. This is called *Anastrophe*. Thus, ἀρετῆς πέρι, *concerning virtue*.

πάρα, for πάρεστι is parox., as is ἔπι for ἔπεστι, and ἔνι for ἔνεστι.

65. ἀνά and διά do not suffer Anastrophe (the former to distinguish it from ἄνα, voc. of ἄναξ, and used also for ἀνάστηθι, the latter from Δία, accus. of Ζεύς), nor ἀμφί, ἀντί.

§ 8. Elision.

66. When an accented final syllable is elided before a word beginning with a vowel, if the elided word is *declinable*, it throws the accent back to the nearest syllable; if *undeclinable*, it loses its accent altogether. The accent thus thrown back will be an *acute*, even though it fall on a syllable long by nature. Thus, λεύκ' ἄλφιτα, for λευκὰ ἄλφιτα : κῆφ' ὅτι, for καὶ εἰπὲ ὅτι, *and say that*— : πόλλ' ἔχων for πολλὰ ἔχων : φήμ' ἐγὼ (not φῆμ' ἐγώ). But παρ' ἐμοῦ (never παρά μου) : ἀλλ' ἔφη for ἀλλὰ ἔφη, *but he spoke* : ἄλλ' ἔφη would be, *he spoke other things.*

67. The term *Prodelision* has been applied to the cutting off a *short* vowel at the beginning of a word, after a *long* vowel at the end of a preceding word. Thus, μή μου 'φέλης, for μή μου ἀφέλης : χρεία 'στι for χρεία ἐστί.

§ 9. Crasis.

68. By Crasis is meant the union of two words, the former of which ends, and the latter begins, with a vowel. A mark (') called the *Coronis*, is placed over the syllable thus contracted, to indicate where the Crasis has taken place. Thus, τἀγαθὰ for τὰ ἀγαθὰ. In such a Crasis as ἃ ἄν = ἃν or ὁ αὐτὸς = αὐτὸς, the Coronis is lost in the breathing. Porson however writes αὐτός.

69. The words that most commonly form a Crasis with a succeeding word are *the article, the neuter relative pronoun,* and the conjunction καί. ἐγὼ also, τοί, μέντοι, ποῦ, ὦ (voc.) frequently stand first in a Crasis.

70. A lenis consonant combined with an aspirated vowel is changed into its corresponding aspirate. Thus, τὰ ἕτερα = θάτερα : τὸ ἱμάτιον = θοἱμάτιον.

71. All the final vowels of the article, in Crasis with (α), coalesce into long α. Thus, ὁ ἀνήρ = ἀνήρ, τοῦ ἄνδρος = τἄνδρος.

72. The αι of καί is frequently elided before a long vowel or diphthong. Thus, καὶ εἰ = κεἰ : καὶ ἦλθον = κἦλθον.

P

106

73. **List of Crases most frequently used.**

τὰ ἐμά	=	τἀμά.	τοῦ ἐτέρου	=	θατέρου.
τὰ ὅπλα	=	θὤπλα.	οὗ ἕνεκα	=	οὕνεκα.
καὶ ἐγώ	=	κἀγώ.	ὅτου ἕνεκα	=	ὅθούνεκα.
καὶ ἡ	=	χἠ.	τοῦ ἐστιν	=	τοὗστιν.
καὶ ὅσα	=	χὤσα.	ὃ ἄνερ	=	ὦνερ.
καὶ εἶτα	=	κᾆτα.	ἐγὼ οἶδα	=	ἐγᾦδα.
καὶ οἶνος	=	κῷνος.	τὸ ἔργον	=	τοὖργον.
ἡ ἀρετὴ	=	ἁρετή.	οἱ ἐμοὶ	=	οὑμοί.
τῇ ἡμέρᾳ	=	θἠμέρᾳ.	ὁ ἀνὴρ	=	ὡνήρ. (Ion.)
ὁ ἐπὶ	=	οὑπί.	τὸ αὐτὸ	=	τωὐτό. (Ion.)
τὸ ὄνομα	=	τοὔνομα.	τὸ ἀληθὲς	=	τὰληθές. (Ion.)
τὸ ὕδωρ	=	θοὔδωρ.	τοῦ ἄλγεος	=	τὤλγεος. (Dor.)
μέντοι ἄν	=	μέντἄν.	ὁ ἐξ	=	ὡξ. (Dor.)
οἱ ἕτεροι	=	ἅτεροι.	καὶ ἐὰν	=	κἤν. (Dor. and Ion.)
τοῦ ἀνθρώπου	=	τἀνθρώπου.	χὥδωνις	=	καὶ ὁ Ἄδωνις.
τοι ἄρα	=	τἄρα.	τοι ἄν	=	τἄν.

74. By *Synizesis* two syllables of the *same* word are pronounced and scanned as one: thus πόλεως is pronounced πόλως. The cases of θεὸς are frequently thus contracted in the Greek plays.

75. By *Syneophonesis* two syllables of *different* words are pronounced (though not written) as one. Thus, ἢ οὐ, μὴ οὐ, are pronounced as single words. So with ἐπεὶ οὐ, ἐγὼ εἰμί.

§ 10. Compounds.

76. A word in *Synthetical* composition (*i.e.* where two words coalesce, with some change, into one) throws back its accent as near the first word as possible. Thus, Διόγνητος, λεοντόφωνος, φιλόσοφος.

77. A word in *Parathetical* composition (*i.e.* where two words merely stand *side by side* without change), usually

takes the accent of the second word, as in Κορακοσπέτρα, ὑοσκύαμος. (Cf. Goettling p. 370 § 55.) So in pronouns compounded with οὖν, as ὁστισοῦν, and in adverbs, as ταπρῶτα, οὐκέτι, δηλαδή, δηλονότι, &c.

78. If the second of two words parathetically compounded be an enclitic, the first retains its original accent, even when the enclitic is long by nature. Thus, ἤτοι, ἦτοι, μήτις, ἦπου, εὖτε, &c. If the first word be a proclitic, the compound is parox., as in ὅσπερ, εἴτε, αἴθε, οὕτις, &c.

79. Words compounded of κτείνω, τίκτω, and τρέφω, if active in signification, are parox., if passive, proparox. (See Rule 38.)

80. Words compounded of ἡγέομαι, ποιέω, ἀμείβω, are oxyt.: as στρατηγός, ἀργυραμοιβός.

§ 11. Proclitics or Atonics.

81. There are a few monosyllabic words having no accent, and therefore called Atonics, which Hermann has called *Proclitics*, because they as it were *incline forward* to the followin g word, and form part ofit.

82. These are the articles ὁ, ἡ, οἱ, αἱ, the conjunctions εἰ, αἱ, and ὡς *as:* the particle οὐ or οὐκ; and the prepositions ἐκ (ἐξ), εἰς (ἐς, ὡς), ἐν (εἰν) but not ἐνί.

83. Thus, ὁ πατήρ is accented as though it were a single word ὁπατήρ: οὐ λέγω, as if οὐλέγω: ὡς ἔφη as if ὡσέφη, &c.

84. ἐξ may be used after its case: it is then oxyt., as κακῶν ἔξ: εἰς and ἐν are also thus used, but only rarely, by Epic writers: for the latter form ἐνὶ is usually thus employed, and, by Anastrophe, accented ἔνι.

85. οὐ at the end of a clause, ὡς used for οὕτως *thus*, and after the word to which it refers, and the article ὁ when it

108

stands for the relative ὅς, are oxyt. Thus, ἀγαθὸς μὲν, σοφὸς δ' οὔ: ὡς ἔφη, *thus he spake*: θεὸς ὥς, *as a god*: κλῦθί μοι ὃ χθιζὸς ἤλυθες (Hom.) *hear me thou who camest yesterday.*

§ 12. Enclitics.

86. Enclitics are words which *incline backwards* to the preceding word, and are pronounced as if they formed part of it. Some of them are monosyllables, others dissyllables.

87. The enclitics are—1. The present tenses of φημὶ and εἰμί (exc. 2 pers. sing. φής, εἶ).

2. The following cases of the three personal pronouns— μοῦ, μοί, μέ: σοῦ, σοί, σέ: οὗ, οἷ, ἕ, σφέ, νίν, μίν: σφωΐν, σφίσι, with the Ionic forms σφωέ, σφέων, σφέας.

3. The indefinite pronoun τίς, τί, τινός, &c. in all its cases and numbers, with the abbreviated forms τοῦ, τῷ, for τινός, τινί. The indefinite adverbs πώς, πώ, πή, πού, ποθί, ποθέν, ποί, ποτέ. All these, when used *interrogatively*, are accented, the monosyllables with cmflx., the dissyllables parox. Thus, τίς ; τί ; πῶς ; πού ; πότε ;

4. The particles τέ, τοί, γέ, νύν, πέρ, θήν, κέ or κέν, νύ, ῥά, and the inseparable particle, δε.*

88. When the word preceding an enclitic is proparox. or properisp. it receives an acute on the last syllable, besides its proper accent. Thus, ἄνθρωπός ἐστι, σῶμά τι.†

---

* The particle δε, when affixed to names of places and forming with them adverbs of motion, follows the general rules laid down in Rule 92. Thus, οἰκόνδε, ἐρεβόσδε, Ἀθήναζε (for Ἀθήνασδε.) But when it is used to strengthen demonst. pronouns or adverbs, it draws the accent to the penult. Thus, τοσόσδε, τοσῷδε, τοιόσδε, τοισίδε.

† When a properisp. word ends in ξ or ψ, it does not receive the incli- nation. Thus, αὖλαξ μου, κῆρυξ ἐστί, as in the case of parox. words, Rule 89.

89. If the preceding word be parox., no change of accent takes place in it, and the enclitic retains its proper accent, if a dissyllable, and loses it, if a monosyllable. Thus, λόγος ἐστί, ἀνθρώπων τινῶν, λόγος τις.

90. If the preceding word be oxyt., the acute accent is retained, and the accent of the enclitic lost. Thus, θήρ τις, καλός ἐστι.

91. If the preceding word be perisp., the accent of the enclitic, whether it be a monosyllable or a dissyllable, is lost. Thus, σοφῶν τινων, φῶς τι, φῶς ἐστι.

28. In all these cases the general laws of accentuation are observed. Thus, in Rule 88, ἄνθρωπός ἐστι being regarded as one word, a *second* accent is necessary on its antepenult., for otherwise the only accent on the word would be on the fifth syllable from the end. So in σῶμά τι = σόομά τι, it would be on the fourth syllable; whereas, by Rule 20, the accent cannot go back beyond the antepenult. In Rule 89, λόγος ἐστί being regarded as one word, the second accent is retained for the same reason, whereas in λόγος τις, another accent is not needed, nor indeed *could* two sharp tones come together. So also, in Rule 90, in καλός ἐστι, the accent is in its proper place as proparox. To make the same remark apply to Rule 91 (in the case of a perisp. word followed by a *dissyllabic* enclitic) we must adopt the rule laid down by grammarians, that " a " perisp. if joined to a dissyllabic enclitic is regarded as an oxytone; and " the final syllable of the enclitic, if long, is considered as short." This appears in the form ὧντινων.

93. All enclitics at the beginning of a sentence retain their accent. Thus, φησὶν αὐτός : σοῦ γὰρ κράτος μέγιστον : τινὲς λέγουσιν.

94. In the case of a number of enclitics succeeding each other, the rule, as stated in the grammars, is that the accent of each is inclined back on the preceding word. Thus, ἄνθρωπός τίς πού ἐστιν : τοῦτό γέ σοί ποτέ φησιν. This,

110

however, contradicts the principle laid down in Rule 92, and some critics more correctly hold that one or more words should be formed from such a series of enclitics, and accented accordingly. Thus, (e. g.) ἄνθρωπός τις μοι (one parox. and one proparox.) καλοί γε τινές εἰσι (two proparox.) φιλεῖ ποτέ τις (one properisp. and one parox.) Thus certainly the anomaly is avoided of a number of sharp tones following each other. (Jelf's Gr. vol. I. p. 62.)

95. φημί retains its accent when separated by a stop from the preceding word. Thus, ταῦτα, φημί, κακά ἐστι.

96. ἐστι is parox.—1. At the beginning of a sentence, as ἐστι κακός. 2. When it denotes existence emphatically, as ἐστι Θεός. 3. When put for ἔξεστι, *it is lawful:* as in ἐστιν ἰδεῖν. 4. When it follows ἀλλ', εἰ, οὐκ, μή, ὡς, καί, μέν, ὅτι, ποῦ, and the pronoun τοῦτ', as τοῦτ' ἐστι.

97. The pronouns σοῦ, σοί, σέ, οἷ, σφίσι, retain their accents—1. When governed by an accented preposition, as in παρὰ σοῦ, περὶ μοῦ, ἐπὶ σοί. (The *unaccented* prepositions unite with the enclitics and take their accents. Thus, ἔν σοι, ἔκ σου, ἔς σε.) 2. After copulative and disjunctive conjunctions, and in an Antithesis. Thus, ἐμὲ καὶ σέ : ἐμοὶ, οὐ σοί.

98. The forms οὗ, οἷ, ἕ, are accented only when they have the force of *reflexive* pronouns.

99. ἔγωγε, ἔμοιγε, ἔμεγε are regular. The oblique cases of σύγε are not enclitic, as in καὶ σέγε.

100. Lastly—enclitics are accented when the syllable which would have received their accent is elided. Thus, καλὸς δ' ἐστί, for καλὸς δέ ἐστι, σῶμ' ἐστὶ, for σῶμά ἐστι.

List of some words of frequent occurrence, which are distinguished only by their accents and breathings, being otherwise written alike.

ἀγός, a leader : ἄγος, a curse.

ἄγων, pres. part. of ἄγω : ἀγών, a contest.

ἀληθές, truth : ἄληθες ; indeed ? really ?

ἄλλα, other things : ἀλλά, but.

ἄρα, then, but : ἆρα, whether ? ἀρά, a prayer.

αὕτη, fem. of οὗτος : αὐτή, of αὐτός.

βασίλεια, a queen : βασιλεία, a kingdom.

βίος, life : βιός, a bow.

βρότος, clotted blood : βροτός, mortal.

δῆμος, people : δημός, fat.

εἶμι, ibo : εἰμί, sum.

εἷς, one : εἶς, 2 aor. part. of ἵημι : εἷς, es : εἰς, prep.

ἕν, one : ἐν, prep. : ἕξ, six : ἐξ, prep.

ἡ, art. : ἥ, relative : ᾗ dat. fem. rel. : ἦ, imperf. of εἰμί or φημί, or surely : ᾖ, subj. of εἰμί : ἤ, or.

ἤδη, now : ᾔδη, noverat.

θέα, a spectacle : θεά, a goddess.

ἴασι, they go : ἰᾶσι, they send.

κάκη, misfortune : κακή, fem of κακός.

κάλως, a cable : καλῶς, bene.

κἄν = καὶ ἐν : κἂν = καὶ ἐάν.

κεῖνος, ille : κεινός, empty.

κῆρ, the heart : κήρ, fate.

νόμος, a law : νομός, *a district.*

ξένων, gen. pl. of ξένος : ξενών, *a guest chamber.*

οἶος, *solus :* οἷος, *qualis.*

οἱ, *these :* οἵ, *who* (rel.) : οἷ, *where :* οἴ, *oh!*

οἱ, dat. of οὗ.

οἶδε, *these :* οἶδε, *he knows.*

οἴκοι, *at home :* οἶκοι, *houses.*

ὅμως, *nevertheless :* ὁμῶς, *together.*

οὗ, *where :* οὐ, *not.*

πείθω, *I persuade :* πειθώ, *persuasion.*

σίγα, *be silent :* σῖγα, *silently :* σιγᾷ, *he is silent.*

φόρος, *tribute :* φορός, *fruitful.*

φῶς, *light :* φώς, *a man.*

ψύχη, pl. of ψῦχος, *cold :* ψυχή, *the soul.*

ὤν, gen. pl. of ὅς, *qui :* ὤν, pres. part. of εἰμί.

ὦν, Ionic form of οὖν.

ὦμος, *a shoulder :* ὠμός, *raw.*

PART VI.

\

GREEK IDIOMS.

1. οἱ μὲν—οἱ δέ, *some—others.*

2. τὸ μὲν—τὸ δέ,—*partly—partly.*

3. τῇ μὲν—τῇ δέ, *here—there ; in one respect——but in another : τῷ, on this account.*

4. τὰ τῆς τύχης, *the dispensations of fortune.*

5. οἱ πολλοί, *the greater number : the common people : οἱ ὀλίγοι, the Oligarchy.*

6. ἡ ἄλλη Ἑλλάς, *the rest of Greece.*

7. τὸ λέγειν, *speaking : τοῦ λέγειν, of speaking, &c.* (Lat. dicere, dicendi, dicendo,) &c.

8. οἱ πάλαι ἄνθρωποι, *the men of old : ἡ ἄνω πόλις, the upper city.* (Article with Adverbs.)

9. τὸ πρῶτον, *for the first time : τὸ τελευταῖον, lastly : τὰ πολλά, mostly : τὸ λοιπόν, for the future.*

10. τὰ δύο μέρη τῶν τριῶν, *two parts of three.*

11. δέκα ταῖς πάσαις ναυσίν, *with ten ships in all.*

Q

114

12. ὁ Σωκράτης, the (well-known) Socrates.

13. ὁ Ἀσσύριος, the king of Assyria : ἡ Κίλισσα, the Queen of Cilicia.

14. νὺξ ἡ ἡμέρα ἐγένετο, day became night. (Article with the subject.)

15. ὄξυν ἔχει τὸν πέλεκυν, the axe which he has is sharp : ἀκροῖς τοῖς ποσί, on tip-toe. The emphasis here falls on the adjectives.

16. ὁ Κῦρος τρία ἡμιδαρεικὰ τοῦ μῆνος τῷ στρατιώτῃ ὑπισχνεῖται, Cyrus promises three half darics per month to each soldier. (The distributive use of the Article.)

17. τὰ Τρωϊκά, the Trojan war : τὰ Ἑλληνικά, the Grecian history.

18. οἱ κολακεύοντες for οἱ κόλακες, flatterers.

19. τὸ τῆς ὀργῆς, anger.

20. τὰ τῶν θεῶν, the reverence towards the gods.

21. οὗτος ὁ ἀνήρ, or ὁ ἀνὴρ οὗτος, this man : (not ὁ οὗτος ἀνήρ.)

22. αὐτὸς ὁ ἀνήρ, or ὁ ἀνὴρ αὐτός, the man himself : ὁ αὐτὸς ἀνήρ, the same man.

23. ὁ Ξενοκλείδης στρατηγὸς ἦν, πέμπτος αὐτός, Xenoclides was general, himself the fifth, (i.e. with four others.)

24. πολλαὶ θεραπεῖαι τοῖς ἰατροῖς εὕρηνται, many cures have been invented by physicians. (Dat. of agent is used after perf. and pluperf. pass. With other pass. tenses, ὑπὸ, παρὰ, πρὸς, ἐξ, ἀπό, governing gen. are generally used.)

25. ἐγὼ φθονοῦμαι, I am envied : ἐγὼ πιστεύομαι, I am trusted : ἐκεῖνος κατεψηφίσθη, he was condemned. (The object,

which was in gen. and dat. with the active, may become the subject of the passive—unlike the Latin, where *mihi creditur*, not *credor* is used.

26. οἱ Κορίνθιοι ταῦτα ἐπεσταλμένοι, *the Corinthians were charged with these things.* (Passive governing an accusative.)

27. λούομαι, *I wash myself*: ἐποιήσατο θώρακα, *he got a breastplate made*: ἐδιδάξατο τὸν υἱόν, *he had his son taught*: κατεστρέψατο τὸν Μῆδον, *he reduced the king of the Medes under his power.* (Usages of the middle voice.)

28. The second perfect (perf. midd.) usually signifies an *abiding condition*, or *continuance* of the action indicated by the Active form. Thus, πέποιθα, *I am confident*: ἐγρήγορα, *I am awake*: πέπηγα, *I am fixed*: ὄλωλα, *I am ruined*, &c.

29. ὁ Κλέαρχος ἐβιάζετο τοὺς στρατιώτας ἰέναι, *Clearchus tried to force the soldiers to go.* (Usage of the imperfect, *quod agere volebat.*)

30. N.B.—The particle ἀν is never used with the imperative, nor can it be clearly shewn that Attic writers ever used it with the primary tenses of the indicative.

31. ἐποίουν ἀν ταῦτα, *I used to do this.* (Usage of imperfect with ἀν—*quod agere solebam.* Gr. Gr. § 41.)

32. ἡδέως ἀν ἀκούσαιμι, *I should be glad to hear.*

33. βουλοίμην ἀν, *I could wish*: ἐβουλόμην ἀν, *I could have wished.*

34. μακρὸν ἀν εἴη μοι λέγειν, *it would take too long to tell.* (Lat. *longum est dicere.*)

116

35. τόσον ἂν οἴει εὑρεῖν τὸν δόμον πωλούμενον, *how much do you think the house would fetch if sold.* (ἂν with infinitive, denoting *conjectural probability.*)

36. ἂν with the participle has the same force—Thus, αἰτεῖ μισθὸν κ.τ.λ. ὡς οὕτω περιγενόμενος ἂν τῶν ἀντιστασιαστῶν (Xen.) *he demands pay, &c. as though he were likely thus to overcome those of the opposite faction.* .

37. πῶς ἂν ὀλοίμην, *would that I could die!*

38. οὐκ ἂν φθάνοις τοῦτο ποιῶν, *you cannot do this too quickly* : *i.e. do it as quickly as possible.*

39. In conditional sentences, the conditional clause (*i.e.* that containing εἰ or ἐὰν) is called the *Protasis :* the consequent clause, the *Apodosis.*

40. εἴ τι ἔχει, δίδωσιν, *if he has anything, he gives it :* εἴ τι ἕξω, δώσω, *if I shall have anything, I will give it.* (Here the assumption is *objectively certain.* Indicative in both clauses.)

41. ἐάν τι ἔχω, δώσω, *if I have anything, I will give it.* (Here the assumption is *objectively uncertain.* Usually ἐάν with subjunctive in the Protasis, and the future in the Apodosis.)

42. εἴ τι ἔχοις, δοίης ἄν, *if you had anything, you would give it.* (Here the assumption is *subjectively uncertain :* εἰ with optative in the Protasis, and optative with ἂν in the Apodosis.)

43. εἴ τι εἶχεν, ἐδίδου ἄν, *if he had anything, he would give it :* εἴ τι ἔσχεν, ἔδωκεν ἄν, *if he had had anything, he would have given it.* (Here the assumption is *objectively untrue :* εἰ with imperf. or aor. indic. in the Protasis : ἂν with imperf. or aor. indic. in the Apodosis.)

44. μὴ κλέπτε (pres. imper.) *do not steal* (as a habit) : μὴ κλέψῃς (aor. subj.) *do not steal* (a particular thing at a particular time.)

45. οὐ μὴ γράψεις, *don't write, pray* : οὐ μὴ γράψῃς, *you shall not write.* (In the first of these phrases the construction is *will you not not write?* in the second understand δέος ἐστί.)

46. οἶσθ' οὖν ὃ δρᾶσον, or οἶσθ' οὖν ὡς ποίησον, *knowest thou what thou must do?* (A blending of interrogation and command : lit. *knowest thou what? (how?)—do it.*)

47. λέγοις ἄν, *thou mightest say* (nearly *say!* imper.)

48. τί οὖν οὐ διηγήσω ἡμῖν τὴν ξυνουσίαν, *give us, then, an account—or—why don't you give us an account, of the interview?* (where the speaker, in the urgency of his request, speaks of it in the past tense, as though it were already granted.)

49. ἀσκητέον (ἐστίν) ἡμῖν τὴν ἀρετήν, *we must practise virtue:* ἐπιχειρητέον (ἐστίν) ἡμῖν τῷ ἔργῳ, *we should set about the work.* (Usage of Gerundive as neuter, and governing the case of its verb, as though it were ἀσκεῖν δεῖ, and ἐπιχειρεῖν δεῖ)

50. ἀσκητέα (ἐστίν) ἡμῖν ἡ ἀρετή, *we must practise virtue.* (Gerundive agreeing with noun, as in Lat. *exercenda est virtus.*)

51. εἴπω οὖν σοι τὸ αἴτιον, *shall I then tell you the cause?* (Sub. χρὴ ἵνα : the deliberative subjunctive.)

52. ἴωμεν, *let us go:* μαχώμεθα, *let us fight.* (Subj. in exhortations.)

53. βούλει λάβωμαι δῆτα καὶ θίγω τί σου, *do you wish me then to take hold of you and touch you?* (βούλει with subj. sub. ἵνα.)

54. φέρ', ὦ τέκνον, νῦν καὶ τὸ τῆς νόσου μάθης, *come, my son, and learn the nature of the disease.* (Subj. for imper.)

55. λέγω (λέξω) ἵν' εἰδῆς, *I speak, (will speak) that you may know :* ἔλεγον (ἔλεξα) ἵν' εἰδείης, *I was speaking (spoke) that you might know.* (Observe the sequence of Moods—Subj. after the pres. and fut. Optat. after imperf. and aor.)

56. δέδοικα μὴ θάνῃ, *I fear he will die.*

57. ἐδεδοίκειν μὴ θάνοι, *I feared he would die.*

58. δέδοικα μὴ τέθνηκε, *I fear he is dead.*

59. οὐκ ἔχω ὅποι τράπωμαι, *I know not whither to turn myself :* οὐκ εἶχον ὅποι τραποίμην, *I knew not whither to turn myself.* (See 55.)

60. οὐκ ἐκὼν εἶναι ἁμαρτήσομαι, *I will not err willingly at least.*

61. ἐμοὶ δοκεῖν, *in my opinion.*

62. ὀλίγου δεῖν ἀπέθανε, *he was almost dead.*

63. φὴς ἢ καταρνῇ μὴ δεδρακέναι τάδε, *do you admit or deny having done this.* (Infin. with μὴ after verb of denying.)

64. So οὐκ ἀρνοῦμαι μὴ οὕτως ἔχειν, *I do not deny that it is so.* (μὴ may also be omitted.)

65 μικρὸν ἐξέφυγε τοῦ μὴ καταπετρωθῆναι, *he narrowly escaped being stoned to death.* (Infin. with μὴ after a verb of escaping. Lat. parum abfuit quin—)

66. ὅσον γ' ἐμ' εἰδέναι, *as far as I know.*

67. οὐκ ἔφασαν ἰέναι τοῦ πρόσω, *they refused to advance any further.* (Note πρόσω with the Article.)

68. μεῖζω ἢ κατα δάκρυα πέπονθα, *I have suffered afflictions too great for tears.*

69. οἴομαι εὐδαίμων εἶναι, *I think I am happy.* (Where εὐ- - δαίμων agrees with the subject of οἴομαι, not with that of the infinitive, ἐμὲ understood.)

70. So ἔφη αὐτὸς εἶναι στρατηγὸς, οὐκ ἐκεῖνον, *he said that he (himself) was general, not he* (some other person.)

71. δίκαιός εἰμι τοῦτο ποιεῖν, *I think it right to do this.*

72. νεώτεροί εἰσιν ἢ ὥστε ταῦτ' εἰδέναι, *they are too young to know this.*

73. ἐφ' ἡμῖν ἔσται ἐπιεικέσι καὶ φαύλοις εἶναι, *it will rest with us to be good and bad.* (Dat. with infin.)

74. θαρσῶν νῦν, Διόμηδες, ἐπὶ Τρώεσσι μάχεσθαι, *boldly now, Diomede, fight against the Trojans* (Sub. ὅρα. infin. for imper.)

75. σύνοιδα ἐμαυτῷ εὖ ποιήσας (or ποιήσαντι), *I am conscious of having done well* (where the participle agrees either with the subject of the verb, or with the pronoun.)

76. δῆλός ἐστι κακὸς ὤν, *he is evidently a villain :* ἔλαθεν ἐπιβουλεύων τῇ πόλει, *he secretly plotted against the state.*

77. Verbs of *persevering, beginning, ceasing,* &c. are also used in this construction with the participle.

78. θαυμάσας ἔχω for ἐθαύμασα, *I wondered :* παρὼν ἐτύγχανον for παρῆν, *I was present :* μέν' ὡς κυρεῖς ἔχων, *remain where you are* (for κυρεῖς.)

79. τί μαθὼν τοῦτο ἐποίησας, *what induced you to do this ?* τί παθὼν τοῦτο ἐποίησας, *what possessed you to do this ?*

80. ἐκμαθήσεται ἁμαρτών, *he shall perceive that he has erred.*

81. ὁ λέγων, *he who speaks, the speaker* (Lat. *is qui dicit* :) οἱ μὴ εἰδότες, *they who do not know.*

82 λαβὼν τοῦτον μαστίγωσον, *take this fellow and scourge him :* ὁ δὲ ἀποκριθεὶς εἶπε, *but he answered and said.* (Part. and verb construed by two finite verbs.)

83. ἔπεμψά σε ἀγγελοῦντα, *I sent you with a message.* (Fut. part. signifying *a purpose.*)

84. τί κυπτάζεις ἔχων περὶ τὴν θύραν, *what makes you lurk at the door?* (Observe ἔχων redundant in an interrogative sentence. It is used also without interrogation in this way, as φλυαρεῖς ἔχων, *you are trifling.*)

85. θνῄσκω, παρόν μοι μὴ θανεῖν, ὑπὲρ σέθεν, *I die for you, though it was in my power not to have died.* (Part. used absolutely in accusative : so ἐξόν, δέον, ὑπάρχον, δόξαν, &c.)

86. ἔλεγεν ὅτι δώσοι ἃ εὕροι, or ἔφη δώσειν ἃ εὕροι, *he said he would give what he found* (*Oratio obliqua.* N.B.—φημὶ is usually followed by the accusative with infinitive, λέγω by ὅτι or ὡς.)

87. λέγει ὅτι ἡ ὁδὸς φέρει εἰς τὰς Ἀθήνας, *he says that the road leads to Athens :* ἔλεξεν ὅτι ἡ ὁδὸς φέροι εἰς τὰς Ἀθήνας, *he said that the road led to Athens.* (*Oratio obliqua :* indicative after *present*—optative after *past* tenses.)

88. ἔλεξέ σε, εἰ τοῦτο λέγοις, ἁμαρτήσεσθαι, *he said that you would be wrong, if you were to say this :* (*Orat. obliq.* In oratio recta, it would be—ἐὰν τοῦτο λέγῃς, ἁμαρτήσῃ.)

89. ἔδοξε δ' αὐτοῖς σκέψασθαι, ὅτῳ τρόπῳ ἀσφαλέστατα δια-

πορεύσονται, *they determined to consider in what way they might
pass most safely.* (*Orat. obliq.*: but here the indicative is
used after the historical tense, as in *recta oratio*, the past
being thus vividly represented as the present time of the
speaker.) .

90. φρόντιζε ὅπως μηδὲν κακὸν ποιήσεις, *take care you do
nothing wrong,* (not ποιήσῃς. Thus especially after verbs
denoting *deliberation, anxiety,* and *exhorting.*) So, omitting
the verb, ὅπως μηδὲν ἐρεῖς, *take care you say nothing.* (Vir-
tually an imperative.)

91. πορεύεται ὡς βασιλέα ᾗ ἐδύνατο τάχιστα, *he goes to the
king as quickly as possible.* (Sub. ὁδῷ: observe the *historic
present* πορεύεται in the same sentence with the imperf.
ἐδύνατο.)

92. οἷός τ᾽ εἰμὶ τοῦτο ποιεῖν, *I am able to do this:* (*i.e.* I am
such a man as to do this.)

93. ἔστιν οἵ (Lat. *sunt qui*) seem, by usage, to have
coalesced into one word, with a regular inflexion. Thus,
ἔστιν οἱ φεύγουσι, *some are flying:* ἔστιν οἷς ἐπίστευσε, *he
trusted some:* ἔστιν οὓς ἔβλαψε, *he hurt some.* (Observe ἐστίν,
sing., with οἵ, *plur.*)

94. ἐρῶ οἵου σοῦ ἀνδρός, *I love such a man as you:* φθονέω
οἵῳ σοὶ ἀνδρί, *I envy such a man as you:* &c.

95. So with the phrase οὐδεὶς ὅστις οὐ. Thus, οὐδεὶς οὐκ
ἂν τοῦτο λέγοι, *there is no one who would not say this:* οὐδενὸς
ὅτου οὐ κατεφρόνησε, *he despised every one:* οὐδένα ὅντινα οὐκ
ἔβλαψε, *he injured every one.* 94 and 95 are remarkable
instances of *attraction.*)

96. ἆρ᾽ οὐ, or μῶν οὐ κακὸς εἶ: (Lat. *nonne? are you not a
villain?*

R

122

97. ἄλλο τι ἢ κακὸς εἶ, *are you anything but a villain?* (A stronger and more vehement form for *nonne.*)

98, πότερον κακός ἐστιν ἢ μῶρος, *is he a villain or a fool?* (Lat. *utrum——an?*)

99. πρὶν is used—(1.) With the indicative. Thus, οὐκ ἐτόλμησαν—πρὶν τοὺς στρατηγοὺς ἡμῶν συνέλαβεν, *they dared not—until they had seized our generals:* (Xen.) (2.) With the optative: as ὑποσχόμενος μὴ πρόσθεν παύσασθαι πρὶν αὐτοὺς καταγάγοι οἴκαδε, *promising not to rest before he had restored them to their homes.* (3.) With the subjunctive, with ἄν : as πρὶν ἂν δῶ δίκην, *before I suffer punishment.* (4.) With the infinitive, οὐδ' ὅγε κῆρας ἀφέξει, πρίν γ' ἀπὸ πατρὶ φίλῳ δόμεναι κούρην, *nor will he withdraw the fates before* (Agamemnon) *restores the damsel to her father.*

100. δή, πὲρ, γὲ, are called *strengthening particles.* δή (probably a weakened form of ἤδη,) expresses the *exactness* of the notion of the word to which it belongs. It may frequently be rendered by *just, in sooth, forsooth.* In the phrase καὶ δὴ τεθνᾶσι, it conveys a *supposition—suppose they are dead.* φέρε δὴ, *come now:* οἷα δὴ, *just as:* ὡς δή, *as then:* εἰ δή, *if then:* πῶς δὴ, *how then?* (impatiently.) πὲρ is an enclitic form of περὶ, *thoroughly:* πρῶτόν περ, *quite the first.* It is used for the Latin *cunque* (Eng. *soever*): ὅσπερ, *the very man who:* ὥσπερ, *just as,* &c. γὲ is *intensive.* It adds the kind of emphasis that we give by pronunciation, or printing in italics : κεῖνός γε, he, *I say :* εὖ γε κηδεύεις πόλιν, *you, forsooth, take good care of the city.* It is frequently used in the Tragedians to express *assent.* Thus, Tiresias says, in reply to a question of Œdipus, εἴ περ τί γ' ἐστὶ τῆς ἀληθείας σθένος, *yes! if there is any power in truth.* (Œd. Rex. 370). Διός γε διδόντος, *that is, God willing.*

CPSIA information can be obtained at www.ICGtesting.com
Printed in the USA
BVOW071201280912

301676BV00015B/28/P